Contents

D1353874

Why do historians differ?

THE purpose of the Flagship Historymakers series is to explore the main debates surrounding a number of key individuals in British, European and American History.

Each book begins with a chronology of the significant events in the life of the particular individual, and an outline of the person's career. The book then examines in greater detail three of the most important and controversial issues in the life of the individual – issues which continue to attract differing views from historians, and which feature prominently in examination syllabuses in A-level History and beyond.

Each of these issue sections provides students with an overview of the main arguments put forward by historians. By posing key questions, these sections aim to help students to think through the areas of debate and to form their own judgements on the evidence. It is important, therefore, for students to understand why historians differ in their views on past events and, in particular, on the role of individuals in past events.

The study of history is an ongoing debate about events in the past. Although factual evidence is the essential ingredient of history, it is the *interpretation* of factual evidence that forms the basis for historical debate. The study of how and why historians differ in their various interpretations is termed 'historiography'.

Historical debate can occur for a wide variety of reasons.

Insufficient evidence

In some cases there is insufficient evidence to provide a definitive conclusion. In attempting to 'fill the gaps' where factual evidence is unavailable, historians use their professional judgement to make 'informed comments' about the past.

New perspectives

Changing circumstances in a country's history may have an effect on how historians view the past. In the case of Germany, the rise of Nazism and the subsequent division of the country has led to reinterpretations of the Bismarck era. During the Cold War, historians in East German universities had to work in the context of an official, Soviet-imposed Marxist doctrine. This inevitably determined the way the past was interpreted and presented. The reunification of the country has also been a major influence on today's historians.

A 'philosophy' of history?

Many historians have a specific view of history that will affect the way they make their historical judgements. For instance, Marxist historians – who take their view from the writings of Karl Marx, the founder of modern socialism – believe that society has always been made up of competing economic and social classes. They also place considerable importance on economic reasons behind human decision-making. Therefore, a Marxist historian looking at an historical issue may take a completely different viewpoint to a non-Marxist historian.

The role of the individual

Some historians have seen past history as being largely moulded by the acts of specific individuals. Bismarck, Napoleon I and Cavour are seen as individuals whose personality and beliefs changed the course of 19th-century European history. Other historians have tended to play down the role of the individuals; instead, they high-light the importance of more general social, economic and political change. Rather than seeing Bismarck as an individual who changed the course of political history, these historians tend to see economic growth or social change as the vital factors.

Placing different emphasis on the same historical evidence

Even if historians do not possess different philosophies of history or place different emphasis on the role of the individual, it is still possible for them to disagree in one very important way. This is that they may place different emphases on aspects of the same factual evidence. As a result, History should be seen as a subject that encourages debate about the past, based on historical evidence.

Historians will always differ

Historical debate is, in its nature, continuous. What today may be an accepted view about a past event may well change in the future, as the debate continues.

Timeline: Bismarck's life

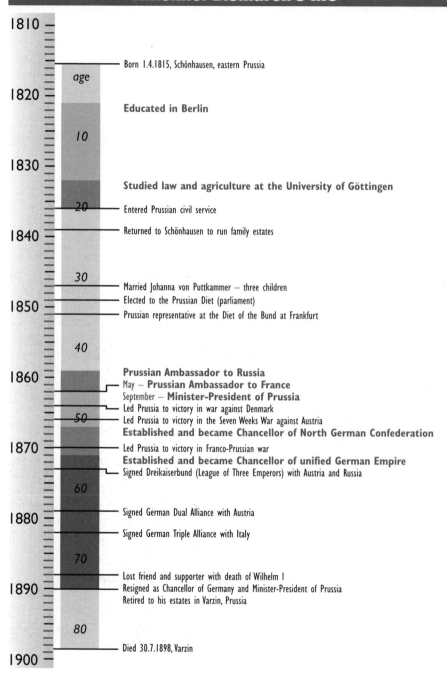

1810

age

Born 1.4.1815, Schönhausen, eastern Prussia

1820

Educated in Berlin

10

1830

Studied law and agriculture at the University of Göttingen

20
Entered Prussian civil service

1840
Returned to Schönhausen to run family estates

30
Married Johanna von Puttkammer – three children
Elected to the Prussian Diet (parliament)

1850
Prussian representative at the Diet of the Bund at Frankfurt

40

1860
Prussian Ambassador to Russia
May – **Prussian Ambassador to France**
September – **Minister-President of Prussia**
50 Led Prussia to victory in war against Denmark
Led Prussia to victory in the Seven Weeks War against Austria
Established and became Chancellor of North German Confederation

1870
Led Prussia to victory in Franco-Prussian war
Established and became Chancellor of unified German Empire
Signed Dreikaiserbund (League of Three Emperors) with Austria and Russia

60

1880
Signed German Dual Alliance with Austria

Signed German Triple Alliance with Italy

70

Lost friend and supporter with death of Wilhelm I
1890
Resigned as Chancellor of Germany and Minister-President of Prussia
Retired to his estates in Varzin, Prussia

80

Died 30.7.1898, Varzin
1900

Chancellor Otto von Bismarck in 1881, a decade after the proclamation of the unified German Empire.

Bismarck: a brief biography

How did he make history?

Otto von Bismarck is one of the most complex and important characters in European history. He was idolised in his time as the creator of a united Germany. He led the German kingdom of Prussia through three successful wars and made it the dominant state in a new German Empire. He made a new constitution for Germany, and his diplomacy was a major factor in European politics for nearly twenty years. He gave Germany modern institutions and made it a major world power. A large, restless and energetic man, he smoked and drank heavily, and relished quarrels. But he was also sensitive, sentimental and highly intelligent, with a superb understanding of international affairs.

From country squire to politician

Junker: a class of Prussian aristocrats.

Bismarck was born into a Prussian **Junker** family at a time when Prussia was the largest kingdom in an ununified Germany. His father was a typical 'country squire', living for his estates and hunting, fishing and shooting. His mother ensured that her son had a good education at school in Berlin, and aged 17 he began his studies in law and agriculture at the University of Göttingen. After an undistinguished period in the Prussian civil service as a judicial administrator, he went back to run the family estates, marrying the 23-year-old Johanna von Puttkammer when he was 32. Despite his many affairs, their marriage was a stable one and they had three children. They remained together until her death in 1894.

Diet: local assembly or parliament.

Oratory: the art of making speeches.

Reactionary: opposed to modern ideas of liberal change and reform.

Liberal: believing in a constitution that guaranteed freedom for the individual in terms of religion, political beliefs and trade.

Public life

In 1849, aged 34, he was elected to the Prussian **Diet**. With his legal training and acute intelligence, it was natural that he should enjoy parliamentary **oratory**. But the side of him that was **reactionary**, intensely monarchist and class-prejudiced rejected the whole concept of **Liberal** parliamentary government. Despising the middle-class liberals in the Prussian parliament, he made it clear that his only interest was the power of the Prussian monarchy. In 1851, aged 36, Bismarck was appointed Prussian representative to the Bund, the Austrian-dominated German Confederation, in Frankfurt.

Frankfurt, St Petersburg and Paris

While at the Bund he pursued an anti-Austrian line, relentlessly championing Prussia as the equal of Austria. His advice to the Prussian cabinet was to take advantage of any Austrian weakness in order to promote Prussian influence. He was made Ambassador to Russia in 1859, aged 44, and was then appointed Ambassador to Paris three years later.

Minister-President

In 1862 Prussia was in crisis. The liberal majority in parliament objected to army reforms proposed by the King of Prussia, **Wilhelm I**. The King insisted that the army reforms were necessary, but was not prepared to destroy parliament and rule by force alone to have them passed. His advisers, particularly **Von Roon**, the Minister for War, advised sending for Bismarck as a 'hard man' to pass the army reforms in the teeth of this intense opposition. Consequently, Bismarck was made Minister-President (prime minister) of Prussia on September 25, 1862, aged 47. The reforms were passed, and he made his position clear in his most famous words: 'It is not by speeches and majority resolutions that the great questions of our time are decided … it is by iron and blood'. This speech later helped earn him the nickname 'Iron Chancellor'. Seeming to despise parliament, Bismarck looked for opportunities to increase Prussia's influence, hoping that success abroad would end opposition at home.

**Wilhelm I
(1797–1888)**
King of Prussia from 1861, as well as Kaiser (emperor) of Germany after 1871. Responsible for a new era of greater freedom in Prussia, he initially opposed the appointment of Bismarck as Minister-President of Prussia. Bismarck gave him complete loyalty but struggled to persuade him on many issues. Though theirs was an uneasy relationship, he did take Bismarck's advice, and Wilhelm's support was a mainstay for Bismarck. Bismarck feared the consequences of Wilhelm's more liberal son becoming Emperor in 1888.

**Albrecht von Roon
(1803–1879)**
A conservative who was devoted to the monarchy, Von Roon was deeply interested in army reform. Minister for War in 1859, he persuaded the King to appoint Bismarck as Minister-President. With Bismarck, he implemented the reforms that made the victories against Denmark, Austria and France possible. He was made a Count in 1871 and was Minister-President of Prussia in 1871–3. He was made Field Marshall in 1873, but retired from public life due to bad health.

Diplomatic success

Duchies: areas ruled over by a duke.

Bismarck was able to show his skills when a quarrel arose over the northern **duchies** of Schleswig and Holstein in 1863. These two provinces had partly German-speaking populations, but were nominally ruled by Denmark. When the Danish king died, it was uncertain whether the duchies should stay under Danish control or pass under German influence and become part of the Bund. Bismarck saw that if Germany took over and the duchies entered the Bund, the gainer would be Austria. Austria had created the Bund and was the dominant power. If Austrian influence grew, it would be to the detriment of Prussia. So, Bismarck persuaded Austria to forget about drawing the duchies into the Bund, and to enter into an equal partnership with Prussia to claim the duchies for themselves. This way, power between Austria and Prussia would be kept equal. Thus, the two powers, acting independently of the Bund, joined forces and waged a successful war against Denmark that brought the duchies under German control.

Convention: treaty or agreement.

The **Convention** of Gastein in 1865 established joint control, with Prussia taking Schleswig and Austria Holstein.

The war against Austria and its aftermath

Bismarck saw how he could use the division of the duchies between the two German powers to generate friction with Austria. This friction proved to be a good enough pretext for going to war with, and breaking free from, Austria. The war lasted seven weeks, with Prussian forces victorious. A quick peace was signed at Prague. Bismarck insisted on taking no Austrian lands and not humiliating Austria by a victory parade. He had been with the Prussian forces and was shocked at the sight of the dead and wounded. Prussia **annexed** some lands of Austria's allies in North Germany, forced the North German states to join Prussia in a new **North German Confederation**, and signed military alliances with the South German states. He had made Prussia the most powerful kingdom in Germany.

Annex: take over another country.

North German Confederation: association of North German states with a new constitution, government and parliament, founded in 1867, which formed the basis of the German Empire in 1871.

Just as there was no humiliation of Austria, so there was no military coup or destruction of the liberal opposition within Prussia. As Bismarck said, 'Genius is knowing when to stop'. He gave the new Confederation a highly democratic constitution. The King of Prussia was the overall ruler and there was a federal government headed by a Chancellor, chosen by the King. This, naturally, was Bismarck, now aged 52.

Understanding Bismarck

Bismarck was a complex, often contradictory figure.

■ A hard-drinking, over-eating, cigar-smoking landowner who was contemptuous of university intellectuals, but who was widely read, deeply affected by music and fascinated by history.

■ A devoted servant of the Prussian King and German Emperor, Wilhelm I, yet bitterly critical of Wilhelm's wife and son (the future Emperor Frederick III), as well as Frederick's son (the future Emperor Wilhelm II).

■ A strict conservative who used force to withstand change, neutralise parliamentary power, and uphold the class interests of Prussian landowners. Yet he introduced one of the most advanced voting qualifications in Europe and a number of innovative social reforms.

■ An anti-liberal 'Iron Chancellor' who has been accused of setting Germany on the path to Nazi dictatorship. Yet he also allied himself with Liberals, pursued forward-thinking policies against the Catholic church, and supported free trade.

■ A great believer in the power of 'iron and blood' to resolve international issues, he was instrumental in waging three wars during the 1860s, yet was shocked by the casualties, and worked tirelessly for peace after 1871.

■ Architect of a new, unified German Empire, yet he was indifferent to its ambitions for much of his career and distrusted popular nationalism.

■ A man contemptuous of fame and popular acclaim, yet who went out of his way to justify himself and create his own legend in his memoirs.

> *'Otto von Bismarck has broken the backbone of the German nation'*
> Contemporary historian Hans Mommsen

The Franco-Prussian War

Bismarck had done his best to ensure that France did not get involved in Prussia's war with Austria in 1866. However, Napoleon III, the French emperor, was disappointed that France had gained nothing from a European conflict of this size.

In an incident that followed in 1870, it appeared that Bismarck was trying to provoke France into war with Prussia. That year he encouraged the Prussian King Wilhelm I's nephew, Leopold of Hohenzollern, to accept an offer to become King of Spain. Predictably, there were protests from the French, who also had their eyes on the throne. On 12 July 1870 Leopold's candidature was withdrawn, but the French public and press were stirred up, and the French Ambassador to Prussia sought an audience with Wilhelm I at the German spa town of Ems. The French wanted a guarantee that not only would Leopold's candidature be withdrawn, but also that it would not happen again. The King was courteous but firm and would not agree. A telegram was sent informing Bismarck of what had happened. Bismarck then edited it to make it appear that the King had spoken angrily to the ambassador, and released it to the press apparently in order to provoke France, which it successfully did. This provided Bismarck with the opportunity to send Prussian forces against France in a war that led the South German states to ally with Prussia. He now had both North and South Germany on his side, and his forces were, again, triumphant.

The Empire

Reich: German word for 'empire'.

With northern and southern states joined, a new, unified German Empire was proclaimed at a ceremony at Versailles in 1871. Wilhelm I was proclaimed Emperor of this new **Reich**, and the 66-year-old Bismarck – arguably the architect of it all – became its Chancellor. Prussia remained the largest state, dominating the government, the army and the administration. As Chancellor, Bismarck watched over a massive commercial and industrial expansion. Helped by federal laws regulating trade, weights and measures and transport, there was considerable economic growth. His tough brand of conservatism, which leaned heavily on military force, soon helped earn him the nickname 'Iron Chancellor'.

Domestic policies

Reichstag: the lower house of the German imperial parliament.

In the **Reichstag** Bismarck had the support of the National Liberals, but faced hostility from the Catholic Centre Party and the SPD

(German Socialist Party). To deaden this hostility, he pursued aggressive policies against them. In the so-called **Kulturkampf**, Bismarck permitted laws against Catholic schools, allowed civil marriage and suppressed religious houses. However, force alone was not likely to succeed. Bismarck understood this enough to try to win working-class support with some social reforms in the 1880s.

Kulturkampf: German for 'the struggle between civilisations'. It came to be applied to the struggle between the German state and the Catholic Church in the 1870s.

Foreign policy

In 1872 Bismarck negotiated the League of the Three Emperors with Russia and Austria – the Dreikaiserbund. He hoped that this would isolate France and that peace in Europe could be kept by stressing the joint interests of Austria, Russia and Germany. But France recovered from the defeat of 1871 quicker than expected, and in 1875 Bismarck began a 'war scare' of threats against her. The response from other countries was critical, and the dangers of Germany becoming isolated by her own agression were clear.

After a series of crises over the Balkans between 1875 and 1878, Bismarck held a great meeting of international leaders in Berlin to try to resolve the problems. This was the Congress of Berlin, and he set himself up as the **'honest broker'**. This was a high point of prestige for the new Germany and for Bismarck personally, but it also led to problems. Though compromise was reached, Russia was angry at failing to secure her aims in the area, and blamed Germany for not helping her.

'Honest broker': a neutral go-between.

Alliances and agreements after 1879

In 1879 Bismarck took what came to be one of the key decisions of his post-1871 career and signed an alliance with Austria, known as the Dual Alliance. He saw the alliance as part of a package of measures that also included an alliance with Italy in 1882 (making the Dual Alliance the Triple Alliance). Again, the Italian alliance was made with the intention of isolating France. Fearing a French alliance with Russia, he revived the Dreikaiserbund and then signed the **Reinsurance Treaty** with Russia in 1887. Bismarck was 72. By a web of alliances, he had kept France isolated, but his hopes for the future were waning.

Reinsurance Treaty: a secret agreement between Russia and Germany. It decreed that each party would remain neutral if either became involved in a war with a third nation, but that this would not apply if Germany attacked France or if Russia attacked Austria.

Two new Emperors and Bismarck's fall

The heir to the throne of the German Empire, Wilhelm I's son Frederick, admired British **constitutional monarchy**, and was known to wish to move Germany towards more liberal policies. Bismarck

Constitutional monarchy: system of government in which a monarch shares power with an elected assembly.

**Wilhelm II
(1859–1941)**
Kaiser of Germany from 1888 to 1918, Wilhelm was an arrogant man who had visions of German world domination. He set out to strengthen Germany's military and naval forces, even though this damaged Bismarck's carefully-crafted relations with Britain, France and Russia. After Bismarck's resignation, his actions went unchecked and helped to bring about the First World War. He abdicated two days before the Armistice (1918), and went into exile in Holland.

looked forward to Frederick's reign with gloom, but after Wilhelm I's death, Frederick III ruled only for a few weeks and died of cancer in 1888. Frederick's liberal attitudes were not inherited by his son, **Wilhelm II**, who wanted a more dynamic foreign and colonial policy. Bismarck did not agree with this, either. Moreover, the young Kaiser did not like the older man's cynicism and condescension. In 1890, the 75-year-old Bismarck resigned as Chancellor of the German Empire and Minister-President of Prussia.

Last years

Angry and frustrated, he retired to his estates in Varzin, and immersed himself in country pursuits and eating and drinking on a grand scale. He also wrote his memoirs, which contributed greatly to the construction of his own 'legend'. However, he remained concerned about the direction of Wilhelm II's Germany. His increasing pessimism worsened with the death of his wife when he was 79. He died at his estates on 30 July 1898, aged 83.

Bismarck at his estates in Varzin, Prussia, after his resignation as Chancellor in 1890. Bitter about his treatment by Wilhelm II, and anxious for the future of Germany, he spent his time in the aristocratic pursuits of his Junker world.

1

Was Bismarck the key to German unification?

Did he have a plan?

How important was his role in the wars against Denmark, Austria and France?

Was he alone responsible for unification?

Framework of events

1862	Bismarck becomes Minister-President of Prussia
	Prussia rejects Austrian proposal to reform the German Confederation (Bund)
1863	Prussia signs Alvensleben Convention with Russia to co-operate against Polish rebels
	Bismarck prevents Wilhelm I from attending Austrian-sponsored Congress of German Princes
1864	Joint Austrian and Prussian war against Denmark over the Schleswig and Holstein issue
1865	Gastein Convention divides administration of Schleswig and Holstein between Austria and Prussia
1866	Seven Weeks' War between Austria and Prussia
	Prussian victory at Sadowa (Königgrätz)
	Peace of Prague
1867	Luxemburg crisis
	First elections for the new North German Confederation
1869	Failure of negotiations for a Franco-Austrian alliance against Prussia
1870	June Announcement of Prussian prince's acceptance of candidacy for the throne of Spain (Hohenzollern candidature)
	July Meeting between French ambassador Benedetti and Wilhelm I; Ems Telegram
	July Start of Franco-Prussian War
	September Prussian victory at Sedan
1871	January German Empire proclaimed at Versailles
	May End of Franco-Prussian war and Treaty of Frankfurt

EBATE on unification has focused on whether it came about through a planned process devised by Bismarck, master statesman and manipulator, or whether it was the result of longer-term social and economic factors.

The events of unification seem to unfold inevitably, like a story. It was Bismarck who saw the importance of pushing on with military reforms at all costs to equip Prussia for the eventuality of establishing a new state. One of his most famous speeches, in the Budget Commission of the Prussian Diet in September 1860, prepared the way for this:

'It is not by speeches and majority resolutions that the great questions of our time are decided … it is by iron and blood'.

This seemed to establish the direction of policy: the new Germany would be made by war. He showed diplomatic insight by gaining Russian and French neutrality so that he could conduct European affairs unhindered by the great powers of the time. Then the war against Denmark over Schleswig and Holstein not only established the idea of force, but also offered the opportunity to begin Prussia's long-awaited war with Austria. Bismarck was still looking to the future, though. His lenient treatment of Austria after Prussia's victory was to ensure her future support in the war against France. This war, in turn, was necessary to establish the security and European supremacy of a new Germany. Bismarck was confident that his forces would defeat France, and he bided his time until he was able to use the **Hohenzollern** candidature for the Spanish throne to lure France into conflict. This war, by bringing the South German states into alliance with the North, ensured the unification of Germany and the triumph of the new Reich. It looks remarkably well planned.

L. C. B. Seaman's *From Vienna to Versailles* (1955) summarised this version of events as a story 'we are often asked to believe', based as it was on Bismarck's own account in his memoirs and on many biographies. However, Seaman challenged both the 'master plan' idea and indeed the whole concept of 'German unification', pointing out that a more complete unification had to wait until Hitler's **Third Reich**. One historiographical problem is that much of the early writing about unification had been in the form of biographies of Bismarck. Naturally, these put Bismarck at the centre of events. However, there have been some refinements since. The German historian Otto Pflanze in *Bismarck and the Development of Germany* (1963) has spoken of Bismarck having 'a strategy of alternatives'. Equally, A. J. P. Taylor's *Bismarck: Man*

Hohenzollern: family name of the Prussian royal family.

Third Reich: the Nazi regime under Hitler, 1933–45. The German Empire of 1871–1918 was known as the Second Reich.

Landmark Study   The book that changed people's views

A. J. P. Taylor, *Bismarck: Man and Statesman* (Hamish Hamilton, 1958)

Taylor's biography had a similar title to the 1943 biography by the German historian Arnold Oscar Meyer, but the approach was very different. Taylor did not offer the detailed analysis of other historians before and after, but he offered challenging insights. He saw Bismarck not as the master planner, but as a flawed leader driven by circumstances, unsure of his direction and having to make the most of situations as they arose. Much research has been done since 1958, and there has been considerable criticism of Taylor's book, but it still offers a readable and penetrating view of the interaction between the statesman and his times. Taylor's views can be discussed and considered in the light of more modern interpretations that have developed his basic concept.

and Statesman (1958; see **Landmark Study**, above) presents Bismarck as having broad aims to make Prussia rather than Austria the dominant power in Germany, but simply responding to circumstances instead of continuously creating them. More recently, it has been fashionable to focus on broad trends in German history rather than to discuss how far one man dictated events. Bruce Waller's survey of Bismarck historiography in *The Historian* (2002) gives a useful short guide to this.

The newly-unified German Empire, in 1871.

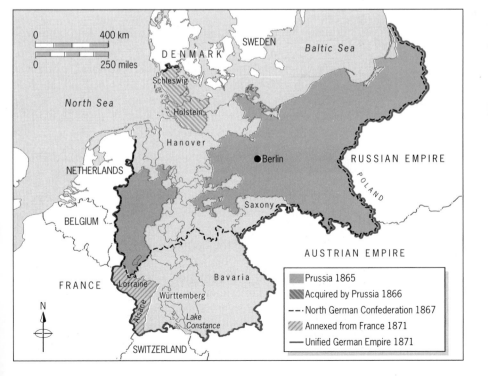

▨	Prussia 1865
▧	Acquired by Prussia 1866
– – –	North German Confederation 1867
▨	Annexed from France 1871
——	Unified German Empire 1871

Did Bismarck have a plan?

There is certainly evidence that, having read the situation within the German Confederation (Bund), Bismarck saw that Austrian supremacy could and should be weakened. As an ambassador, he had watched European affairs closely and made a careful analysis of the way that changes might help to increase Prussia's influence. He saw that the breakdown of the relationship between Austria and Russia over the **Crimean War** opened the door for a change in the existing situation in Germany without the threat of Russian intervention. This suggested that, given the right pressure at the right time, Austria's domination of the Bund could be weakened, for Russia would be unlikely to back her. The main line of debate has been about the *extent* of Bismarck's plan. All these factors offered possibilities, but how far did Bismarck really intend to go? Was he envisaging a Prussian-dominated German state or did he merely want to establish Prussia as an equal partner with Austria?

Crimean War (1853–6): fought by Britain, France and the Ottoman Empire (Turkey) against Russia to prevent supposed Russian expansion.

Bismarck expressed what seemed to be a highly ambitious view in one of his ambassadorial dispatches of 1859. In the event of Austrian involvement in a war against France, he said Prussia 'should march southwards with our entire army, carrying frontier posts in our packs. We can plant them either on Lake Constance, or as far south as Protestantism is the dominant faith' (see map, p. 17). In other words, he seemed to have in mind a conquest of the protestant areas of Germany while Catholic Austria was distracted. When read in combination with his 'iron and blood' speech three years later, these words seem to show prior intent for war on Bismarck's part. In December 1862 he told the Austrian Ambassador to Prussia, 'If Austria persists and restricts the air we breathe, you will conjure up catastrophes, which in the last analysis must end in a fight'.

Quotations like these can be used to build a case for Bismarck intending a showdown with Austria and being intent on war. Yet doubts remain over whether he wanted only to remove Austrian control over North Germany, or to form a unified state in which Prussia would dominate the German world. In addition, Bismarck himself cast doubts on whether he, or indeed any statesman, was capable of planning and executing a sequence of events in any meaningful way: 'Man cannot create the current of events; he can only float with it and steer'. This more humble comment was at odds with other statements implying that he had indeed 'created' the current of events. His earlier biographers, such as Emil Ludwig (*Bismarck,* 1926) and Friedrich Meinecke (*The German*

Catastrophe, 1946), accepted the notion that Bismarck had a plan for unification. This interpretation was informed by Bismarck's own claim, in his memoirs, that he was following a plan. But we must not take these at face value.

It may be worth considering some more realistic views. First that, by 1862, Bismarck had accumulated enough prejudices, opinions, frustrations and hatreds to determine how he might act (but nothing that necessarily points to a fixed plan). Second, A.J.P. Taylor's basic proposition that, within a broad framework of objectives, Bismarck reacted to events and made the best of them without knowing where they might lead – a view that has been subsequently refined and adapted. Finally, the idea that Bismarck pursued a 'strategy of alternatives', having a number of different possible paths and options. This was set out in Otto Pflanze's *Bismarck and the Development of Germany* (1963), and has been particularly helpful to historians. A summary of writing about Bismarck may be found in Edgar Feuchtwanger's *Bismarck* (2002).

How important was Bismarck's role in the wars against Denmark, Austria and France?

Denmark: the turning point

Bismarck's early moves seem so assured that it must have been easy for admirers to see evidence of a well-planned process. He had apparently attempted to gain Russian support by co-operating against a Polish rebellion. He had persuaded Wilhelm I not to attend a conference initiated by Austria to discuss the reform of the Bund. Bismarck then seemed to be the major manipulator of the notoriously complex situation concerning Denmark that emerged in 1863. But there is also a strong case for Bismarck being driven by events and by the attitude of Denmark.

German national feeling ran high over the duchies of Schleswig and Holstein. Both areas (see map, p. 17) had the King of Denmark as their Duke; both contained large numbers of German-speakers. Holstein was predominantly German-speaking and was inside the German Bund. Schleswig was more of a mixture of German- and Danish-speaking people and was not part of the Bund. When Frederick died in November 1863 his distant relative, Christian, succeeded him. But at the same time, a German, the Duke of Augustenberg, decided to revive a family claim to the duchies and became the hero of the German nationalists. The states of the Bund supported him, knowing that Schleswig and Holstein would be admitted to their organisation if Augustenberg were successful.

Bismarck's Austrian dilemma

Given the complexity of this issue, it is difficult to see Bismarck somehow envisaging it, from the start, as a means of provoking war with Austria. What seems clear is this: he did see that, instead of using the issue against Austria, Prussia could manipulate Austria to undermine the Bund. This meant joining with Austria in an attempt to claim the duchies for themselves, excluding the rest of the Bund totally, and ignoring Augustenberg's claim. Austria agreed. She had little to gain from an upsurge of German nationalism or overturning 1852's international agreement. She was also suspicious of France and happy to unite with Prussia to maintain German security in Europe. The joint invasion of the duchies by Austria and Prussia on 1 February 1864 was a reaction to Danish policy. The aim of the invasion was to prevent Christian incorporating Schleswig, not to install a liberal German claimant. Denmark finally ceded Holstein to Austria, and Schleswig to Prussia, on 1 August 1864.

Prussia and Austria: peaceful cohabitation?

There is a strong argument that after the Danish war Bismarck had everything to gain from a continued agreement with Austria. Together, they would prevent the sort of intervention in German affairs by France, Britain and Russia that had been so humiliating previously. The alternative – war against Austria – would be a large scale and uncertain venture. King Wilhelm I was against it. Moreover, the French, as the dominant European power, had a vested interest in maintaining the existing balance of power in Europe. Even railways and superior Prussian weaponry might not ensure victory quickly enough to avoid French intervention. Bismarck even appealed to the Austrian chief minister, Rechberg, to maintain 'the fresh life of an active common policy'; further, he held out the possibility of Austria entering the **Zollverein** in 1877, when membership would next be reviewed.

Zollverein: a union of German states set up in 1834 that abolished customs duties between members to encourage trade. The dominant member state was Prussia; Austria was not a member.

Bismarck forced to think again

However, a major change in Austrian attitudes to Prussia came with the resignation of Rechberg, with whom Bismarck had been willing to co-operate, in October 1864. This led Bismarck to consider alternatives to a friendly relationship with Austria.

Additionally, he had been heartened by reaction to the Prussian victory over Denmark, which had been very well received at home. He changed tack. He began to promote an agitation within Schleswig and Holstein for their complete annexation by Prussia, and held negotiations with France and Italy over it. This forms part of the argument that Bismarck was reacting to changing events rather than following a plan.

Prussia and Austria on the brink

Brinkmanship: diplomatic technique where countries press a dangerous situation to the limit of safety to test their opponents' will and gain an advantage.

In 1865 Prussia stepped up her demands, asking for control of the military forces in Schleswig and Holstein, and announced the building of a canal (the future Kiel Canal). Prussia turned down a proposal by Austria and the smaller states to give the duchies to Augustenberg. There is little doubt by this period that war was being used as a threat over Austria, and it yielded Austrian concessions in the Convention of Gastein, August 1865. Bismarck's **brinkmanship** had produced good results – Prussia now dominated Holstein, could have a naval base in Kiel and build a canal across the base of the Danish peninsula. By the summer of 1865 the government, King Wilhelm I and the army chief Von Moltke had considered the possibility of war with Austria. Friction still existed between Prussia and Austria because of the latter's continued support for Augustenberg.

Napoleon III (1808–1873)
The nephew of Napoleon I (Bonaparte), he became Emperor of France in 1851. Because he regarded himself as the most important statesman in Europe, his relations with the new, expanded Prussia after 1866 were uneasy. Yet he failed to gain allies. His empire became more liberal in 1870, but his appointment of an anti-Prussian (Gramont) as foreign minister led him into conflict with Prussia over the Hohenzollern candidature for the Spanish throne. War with Prussia soon followed and he was captured at Sedan. He died in exile in England.

Any possibility of a war between Austria and Prussia meant that it would be prudent to remain friendly with France, and Bismarck met **Napoleon III** in October 1865. By 28 February 1866, the war was openly on the agenda of the Prussian Crown Council. Bismarck spoke of Prussia's destiny to be at the head of Germany. Von Moltke urged an alliance with Italy, who wanted to reclaim Venetia from Austria, and the agreement was signed on 8 April. It was valid for three months. On 9 April Bismarck went public with a proposal for a new German parliament to be elected by universal suffrage – every German male over 25 would be able to vote. Prussia seemed to be offering a sort of new deal for Germany, but there was cynicism about Bismarck's motives. It seemed ludicrous that the reactionary enemy of parliament was now the advocate of parliamentary democracy.

The Seven Weeks War with Austria

On 9 June 1866 Prussian troops invaded Holstein. When Austria got Bund support to mobilise forces against the invasion, Bismarck declared the Bund dissolved. A German civil war now began, but the result was not a foregone conclusion. Austria was far from being out-manoeuvred: she had obtained a secret treaty with France on 12 June; her artillery had been greatly improved; and three of the largest states in Germany had sided with her. Yet Prussia gained victory in seven weeks, and Bismarck settled a quick peace at Prague that gave Venetia to Italy and dissolved the Bund. He avoided humiliating Austria. Bismarck did not want a huge celebration of national enthusiasm. Nor did he want to be in permanent fear of Austrian revenge.

France made demands for land in western Germany as compensation for her neutrality, but by that time Bismarck had begun preparations for the new North German parliament. He explained to Napoleon III that he could not grant German land to France, since German national feeling was running so high. Privately he spoke of the **'national swindle'** being useful here. In other words, his desire for a more united Germany was dishonest, and he was only using national feeling as an excuse to deny France more territory and greater influence over Germany.

'National swindle': Bismarck was sceptical about the concept of a 'German' nation, as opposed to individual German states. Here he seemed to take the view that it was a false idea, invented by middle-class theorists.

Was Bismarck responsible for the Franco-Prussian War?

The debate on the responsibility for Prussia's war with France has centred on interpreting the situation after the establishment of the North German Confederation in 1867. One interpretation focuses on the unstable and ambitious French regime, determined to assert its superiority over the new Germany. Gordon Craig (*Germany 1866–1945*, 1978) stresses the importance of **'hawks'** in Napoleon III's cabinet. A. J. P. Taylor (*Bismarck: Man and Statesman,* 1958) sees Bismarck as having no aim other than to be left alone after 1866. The other interpretation is that Bismarck regarded the war as inevitable, that he planned it in the longer term and provoked it in the shorter term, leaving the French little option but to assert themselves. In this interpretation, developments within France are secondary. Otto Pflanze in 1963 saw Bismarck deliberately embarking on 'a collision course' (*Bismarck and the Development of Germany, 1815–1871*).

'Hawks': people who are pro-war.

It is possible to see Bismarck regarding the incorporation of the southern states into his new Germany as an inevitable development of the nation, and a war with France as impossible to avoid. Germany could not be in the perpetual shadow of France and could not go on being only partially united. Older interpretations see both of these as part of a master plan for unification and the substitution

Bismarck is seen in this French cartoon of 1870 as 'sweeping' Germany to war again. The caption reads: 'Here is Bismarck, still with his big broom, who scolds and picks up all of the unwilling Germans. Let's go! Go or die! Faster than that! Or the French will eat your sauerkraut!'

of Germany for France as the dominant power in Europe. Yet Paul Schröder, in the *Short Oxford History of Europe* (2000), writes that these views are 'the most doubtful views [and] are seldom debated'.

What made peace a better option than war for both sides?

- France had no allies. Attempts to sign treaties with Austria and Italy had not been successful. (Austria was now tied to Hungary, and despite having an anti-Prussian prime minister, Beust, it was unlikely that Hungary would approve another war in Germany.)

- The South German states were not in favour of unification with the North, despite their military alliance. In Württemberg and Bavaria, elections for the internal parliaments and the new Zollverein assembly created by Bismarck showed a resurgence of anti-Prussian feeling. This weakened Bismarck's Germany and posed no threat to France.

- The South German states were predominantly Catholic, whereas the North was predominantly Protestant. War with

France might result in bringing the Catholics into Bismarck's North German Confederation, but this was dangerous: one of the major problems after 1867 was increasing tension between Protestant and Catholic. Some Catholics had resisted the call-up to the army in the Rhineland in 1866, and religious hostility had increased since then.

- The North German Confederation had been a success, and it did not need to unify fully with the southern states. Economic bonds and military alliance linked North and South, and this should have been enough. Despite national opinion, there were no real military, economic or strategic pressures for Bismarck to go to war to promote further unity. In any case, even if the South German states were part of a new Empire, it would not bring all German speakers into the Reich – even Hitler did not achieve that.

- There was no certainty that a Franco-Prussian war would be a short affair. France was building up its forces and artillery, as was Prussia, whose military leaders had taken valuable lessons from the defeat of Austria. Yet Bismarck needed it to be a short war. If it was not, there was the danger of Austrian intervention, not to mention the prospect of Russia growing stronger while her two chief European rivals were in prolonged conflict.

- Bismarck's own attitude. His response to the Prussian ambassador in Bavaria who urged action to bring in southern Germany and strike at France is revealing:

> 'Violent events would bring about further German unity. To assume the mission of bringing about a violent catastrophe is another matter. Arbitrary interference in the course of history has never achieved anything but to shake down unripe fruit. That German unity is not yet a ripe fruit is obvious. We can put the clocks forward, but time does not move any faster.'

Additionally, Bismarck had been distressed by the grim realities of the war in 1866 that had left thousands dead or crippled.

Bismarck and the Hohenzollern candidature

A. J. P. Taylor's view in 1958 was that the war with France came about not because either side had long-term plans, but because events overtook them and they were forced to react. This view challenged earlier interpretations, which saw more deliberation in Bismarck's actions. The issue of the candidature for the Spanish throne lies at the heart of the discussion.

It would have been hard for Bismarck to foresee the events in Spain that led to a vacant throne being offered to the Prussian prince, Leopold of Hohenzollern, in 1870. When the offer was made, Bismarck pushed the royal family to accept – but why? Was it for the express purpose of starting a war with France, who surely had her eyes on the throne as well? Or was it simply to see how far Germany might benefit from what might develop from the situation? In other words, did Bismarck have a clear aim or was he trying to gain whatever advantage he could from the circumstances? Was he an assured statesman with a plan or a pragmatic gambler? Even if the view is accepted that after 1867 Bismarck saw more advantages than disadvantages in peaceful coexistence with France, by March 1870 he was pursuing a policy that was clearly going to provoke problems with Napoleon III, if not a war. What had changed?

Long-term reasons for Bismarck's change of attitude to France

There were a few factors that may have influenced Bismarck in the long-term. First, French military preparations could not really be ignored. France was building a reserve of nearly a million men, re-equipping its forces with improved rifles and negotiating for an alliance with Austria. Bismarck had been driven into a sort of arms race. For that he needed approval of the military budget by the North German Confederation Reichstag. To return to the parliamentary struggles of 1862 would not have been feasible, so a highly charged international situation would be desirable to force the issue. Leopold's candidature would certainly achieve that.

Next there was the anti-Prussian hostility shown in the elections in Bavaria and Württemberg. Would the military alliance of North and South hold in the light of this anti-national feeling? Further, would these elections show Napoleon III the possibilities of an Austrian-South German alliance?

Finally there is the crucial question of whether Prussia would gain anything by waiting. Bismarck had given himself a line of retreat by claiming quite falsely that the candidature was a family matter for the Hohenzollerns and not official policy, the candidature offered the possibility of starting a war when Prussia was ready. Bismarck could continue to build Prussian strength until the time was right.

Short-term reasons for Bismarck's change of attitude to France

It has also been argued that short-term events, not long-term intentions, were the key. These views are referred to in D. G. Williamson's *Bismarck and Germany, 1862–1890* (1998). First was the appointment of the hard-line anti-Prussian Gramont as French foreign minister in 1870.

Next there were immediate communications problems concerning the Spanish candidature. The plan was that the announcement of the official acceptance of the offer to take the Spanish throne by Leopold of Hohenzollern should coincide with a meeting of the Spanish parliament, the Cortes. Once the throne had been offered and accepted, there would be little that France could do about it. The challenge would be to a decision already taken and given the approval of the Spanish people, and would be hard to sustain. But because of an error by a clerk, the message was not passed on to the Spanish government, and the Cortes was sent home. This gave Gramont the chance to protest before the candidature had been endorsed by Spain.

Events moved quickly and the issue changed: could Bismarck be seen to retract Leopold's candidature and back down in a humiliating way, accepting French demands not only to withdraw, but to promise not to do it again? He had taken military advice that was reassuring about the outcome of a possible war; he had accepted that war would bring unification; he had been aware of increased French military power; he knew that there was a possibility of a future alliance between France and Austria. There was a case for peace, but also a strong case for appearing to be in charge of events and bringing German public opinion behind war.

The Ems Telegram

On 13 July 1870 – on orders from Gramont – the French Ambassador to Germany, Benedetti, saw Wilhelm I at the spa town of Ems and asked for a guarantee that never again would a German prince claim the throne of Spain. The King politely refused. His report in a telegram was edited by Bismarck to make it appear that the exchange had been an aggressive one on both sides. This was released to the press in order to provoke France.

This famous incident has been seen as Bismarck laying a trap for France. However, how far it was part of a premeditated plan is debated. Without the situation in France, it need not have been a cause for war. Also, the withdrawal of the Hohenzollern candidature

King Wilhelm I of Prussia is proclaimed first Emperor of the new, unified German Empire in January 1871 at Versailles, following the fall of Paris. Bismarck, who became its first Chancellor, is in the centre, dressed in white.

under French pressure had left Bismarck humiliated and potentially likely to be dismissed. The arrival of Benedetti gave Bismarck a chance to regain his position and support in Prussia. By revealing to the world that the French had been threatening, Bismarck put Napoleon III in the wrong, prevented Austria or the South German states supporting him and made Prussia seem the injured party. It rescued Bismarck from an unhappy situation largely of his own making.

Bismarck's mastery of the press release is not debated, but his overall wisdom in promoting the candidature and his general control of events is more open to question. Nevertheless, Prussian forces invaded France only days later. By September they had taken Paris, securing the downfall of France and the eventual unification of Germany. The German Empire was proclaimed at Versailles in January 1871.

Was Bismarck alone responsible for unification?

Even if Bismarck was not the master puppeteer and was far more at the mercy of events, a biographical approach can keep him at the centre of developments. However, history is not necessarily biography. The role of different factors and people can be obscured by approaches that focus on one person. So, what role did factors *outside Bismarck's control* play in unification? This is a very large topic, but we can isolate *some* factors.

Economic strengths and weaknesses

First, the considerable economic growth of Prussia and the relative economic weakness of Austria. For 'iron and blood' to be considered as a solution, there had to be the industry to supply the 'iron', to construct the railways and weapons, for the army to be in a position to shed the 'blood'. Had Austria been economically stronger, the separate development of the Zollverein as a Prussian-dominated economic union might not have taken place. Had its military development been backed by a more robust industry and a higher level of spending, the short war of 1866 – on which so much turned – might have been longer and have had all sorts of consequences. This view is to be found in David Blackbourn, *Germany 1780–1918, the Long Nineteenth Century* (1997). He points out that 'Prussia was always likely to come out on top. Austria not only had chronic financial problems and non-German distractions; it also lagged well behind Prussia in economic development'.

German nationalism

Second, the force of German nationalism. This had its roots in all sorts of cultural, political and intellectual developments that had nothing to do with Bismarck. Although devotion to particular states was often stronger than enthusiasm for 'Germany' and most Germans were still non-nationalist peasants, nationalism was a strong element among the protestant middle classes and a weapon that Bismarck could make use of.

International developments out of Bismarck's hands

Third, international developments that owed nothing to Bismarck and that arguably might have changed the situation without him. John Breuilly argues this neatly in his very useful survey of recent writings *The Formation of the First German Nation-State 1800–1871* (1996). Concerning the war with Austria, he writes that Britain and Russia were always unlikely to intervene; Italy was anxious to secure Venice; French policy was undone by the rapid and unexpected Prussian military success, and 'any ordinary statesman in Berlin bent on war with Austria would not have done significantly worse'.

The Prussian 'war machine'

Fourth, the organisation of the state for war. Military reforms had been initiated by von Roon and Wilhelm I. These were part of a process in which the greater powers were reviewing their bureaucratic and military organisation following the experiences of the Crimean War. Smaller powers, for example Saxony, were left behind and therefore vulnerable. Purely military developments such as the development of Prussian weaponry and the strategic deployment of railways proceeded independently, giving Bismarck the necessary means for success. Studies of military history such as John Gooch, *Armies in Europe* (1980) give prominence to these factors.

The Zollverein

There has been much debate on whether this union was the precursor of national unity, or merely a means of providing revenue that had little impact on either economic development or the growth of unification. Helmut Böhme in *The Foundation of the German Empire* (1971) argued that the Zollverein was an important instrument of Prussian control of the German states and thus of unification, but this has been challenged by others. In fact, James Sheehan in *German History 1770–1866* (1989) argues that the Zollverein was mainly to increase tax revenue, and that its economic and political impact as a factor in bringing about unification was very limited.

Was Bismarck the key to German unification?

1. Read the following extract and answer the question.

> '*Many historians have exaggerated the extent of Bismarck's achievement in laying the groundwork for the war against Austria. Britain and Russia were always unlikely to intervene; Italy was anxious to use the Austro-Prussian conflict to secure Venice; the German nationalist movement looked on with horror, powerless. French intervention was only avoided by unexpected Prussian military success. Indeed, one could argue that any ordinary statesman would not have done significantly worse.*'

(Adapted from John Breuilly, *The Formation of the First German Nation-State, 1800–1871* Palgrave, 1996.)

Using information from the extract above, and from the rest of this book, consider the view that Bismarck's achievements in creating a more united Germany have been overrated.

2. How far was Bismarck merely reacting to events from 1862 to 1870?

Was Germany more Liberal than liberal?

How did he change from 'red reactionary' to founder of the 1867 constitution?

How liberal were his religious and social policies?

Framework of events

1871	Proclamation of new German Empire
1872	Anti-clerical Adalbert Falk appointed as Prussian minister of Culture
	Kulturkampf intensifies
	School Inspection Act
	Jesuit Act
1873	Laws against Catholic Church
	Stock Market crashes
1874	Reichstag elections: National Liberals at peak of strength
	Bismarck assassination attempt
	Civil Marriage Act
1878	Wilhelm I assassination attempt
	Anti-socialist law
1879	Resignation of Falk
	Tariff law
1883	Health Insurance law
1884	Accident Insurance law
1885	Expulsion of Poles and Jews from eastern Prussia
1889	Old Age Pensions law
1890	Bismarck resigns (18 March)

THE new German Empire had universal male suffrage, a constitutional system that held a balance between states' rights and the power of the imperial government, and a strong National Liberal party. However, the question remains as to

The constitution of 1871

The German Empire had a federal **constitution**. This meant that the **Länder** had some responsibility for ruling their own affairs. Still headed by the hereditary princes, they had their own governments, responsible for aspects of domestic policy like policing. They also had their own elections for their own assemblies. The biggest Land (state) was Prussia. It made up about two-thirds of Germany. Bavaria was in a special position as it retained its own monarch and army after 1871.

Yet for the Empire as a whole, there were central institutions. First, there was one overall Kaiser (Emperor), to whom all the princes and the King of Bavaria owed allegiance. This was the King of Prussia. He appointed the Imperial (**Reich**) government, headed by a Chancellor (Prime Minister). Bismarck was thus the Chancellor of Germany but also the Minister-President of Prussia. Bismarck could not be dismissed by anyone except the Emperor-King.

Separate from the government was the Imperial parliament. This had two parts – the Reichstag and the Bundesrat. The Reichstag was elected by all German men over 25. It met in Berlin. Unlike the British House of Commons, this 'lower house' had no prime minister and government that were actually elected. Its responsibilities were to vote on legislation and the imperial budget. The Chancellor had direct authority through the Emperor on matters of foreign policy. Bismarck addressed the Reichstag but was not part of it. Elections were held regularly, but the government could dissolve the Reichstag and bring about elections if it wished. The upper house of the parliament was the Bundesrat: a council of representatives from the states. This gave a voice to state governments within the Empire, but, as the largest state, Prussia had the greatest representation here.

Bismarck needed the co-operation of the Reichstag and Bundesrat in passing legislation and obtaining consent for the federal budget, but he was not directly responsible to them. He was accountable only to the Emperor. In the British system, hostile votes in parliament could result in changes of government. This was not true in Imperial Germany. As in the American constitution, a hostile parliament could obstruct the government, but could not topple it.

Constitution: a set of rules by which a country is run.

Länder: the individual states within the Empire.

Reich: German for 'empire'.

how liberal the nation actually was. At the time these arrangements were seen as 'the fig leaf for absolutism', a way for Bismarck to cover up the naked power of the Prussian monarchical state. Yet some historians have seen them as a more genuine attempt to establish a modern state in which Prussia would consult the smaller states on certain matters.

Was Germany more Liberal than liberal?

Much depends here on the capital letter. In terms of our understanding of the general adjective, 'liberal' can mean tolerant, progressive, and aware of the needs of others. Yet 'Liberal' in nineteenth-century terms signified a certain political standpoint that was not necessarily totally 'liberal'. Being a 'Liberal' meant holding certain more specific beliefs. These included:

● a belief in a parliamentary system that effectively shared power with the government; governments should be responsible to the elected parliament

Free trade: the belief that economic wealth and progress can only take place if there are no customs barriers to trade between nations.

● an association with **free trade** policies and a belief in the power of individual economic enterprise and freedom, unrestricted by the state

● opposition to the Catholic Church's control over religious belief and education. The right to be a Catholic was not challenged. Rather, the right of the Church, or any other institution, to control individual belief was challenged

● the idea that, to work effectively, a Liberal state required active, committed and educated citizens with a stake in the country and an understanding of political life. Liberalism did not necessarily involve a belief in democracy.

What was Realpolitik?

Few of Bismarck's admirers would claim that he shared many of these ideas. Indeed for early biographers that was his strength. His

Realpolitik: the belief that the basis of politics is self-interest, not abstract ideas.

brand of politics was to be admired. It was known as **Realpolitik**. Some admired its supposed emphasis on real, practical national interests rather than loose and woolly 'ideas'. But the term has since come to stand for a cynical disregard for ideals and rights. It still forms part of the modern debate about politics, both nationally and internationally.

Realpolitik, parliament and the Liberals

Had Bismarck not made it clear in his 'iron and blood' speech soon after he came to power in 1862 that parliamentary debates were not enough? He claimed that the Liberals had had their chance to make a Germany based on parliamentary ideas at the time of the **Revolution of 1848–9** and had failed because they lacked military and economic power. For Bismarck, ideals alone were no use.

Bismarck made little secret of his contempt for parliament in his early career. He had defied the constitution between 1862 and 1866 by pushing through his military reforms without parliament's approval. His interest was in Prussian expansion, not vague national aspirations. The 1867 constitution of the North German Confederation put Prussia firmly in control because it reflected Prussia's military and economic strength – real factors, not intellectual fancies. By adopting universal male suffrage he gave support to the state rather than to the Liberals, because the masses had little time for middle-class notions of liberty – they wanted specific, concrete advantages, not ideas. This explains Bismarck's surprising affinity with the Socialist leader **Lassalle**. After 1866 the **National Liberals**, not Bismarck, compromised and accepted Prussian power at the price of political and ideological progress. This was confirmed by their support for the new Empire after 1871.

Prussian domination continued. Bismarck pursued increasingly illiberal policies of persecuting his internal enemies: socialism and Catholicism were repressed; opponents were not reconciled, but labelled 'enemies of the Reich'. Within the state of Prussia itself, the voting system gave more votes and influence to the rich. Even economically there was a swing against Liberalism. Free trade gave way to a **tariff** policy that favoured heavy industry and the old aristocracy. German alliance with Austria in 1879 marked a return to a traditional alignment with a conservative power; the persecution of Poles prefigured later illiberal policies. This looks anything but Liberal or, indeed, liberal.

Revolution of 1848–9: there were revolutions in every major European country, except Britain and Russia, led by middle-class Liberals wanting parliamentary constitutions and national unification. Rulers within Germany were forced to accept a national parliament and representative governments, but the revolutions were short-lived and the rulers were restored by armed force.

National Liberals: the party of the Liberals that supported Bismarck in the Reichstag after 1866. He did not reciprocate their respect and admiration.

Tariff: a customs duty on imported goods.

Ferdinand Lassalle (1825–64)
Working as a lawyer when he met Karl Marx, Lassalle, partly influenced by Marx, developed a theory of state socialism emphasising the role of the state and nationalism. He played a key role in establishing the General German Workers' Association of 1863, the first workers' political party in Germany; this later developed into the Social Democratic party in 1875. Lassalle was killed in a duel over a love affair.

G. W. F. Hegel (1770–1831)
A German philosopher who became one of the most influential thinkers of the nineteenth century, Hegel was a professor in philosophy at the University of Heidelberg, and later at the University of Berlin. He thought that obedience to the state was man's highest duty. His method was taken up by Marx, who thought the Absolute Truth was the true Socialist community. His ideas were also used to justify Fascism and the power of the state.

German Empire: 'ultimate human development' or 'speck of grease in a plate of soup'?

Militarism: exaggerated love and respect for all things related to the armed forces.

Wilhelmine: referring to the reign of Kaiser Wilhelm II, 1888–1918.

Antihero: an important figure whose bad characteristics assume such proportions that they become 'heroic' – the opposite of a hero, but not just a villain or a bad person.

Instead of parliament developing, it seemed to be stifled. The federal system was condemned as a sham. **Militarism** grew. Bismarck's Germany seemed to provide the necessary preconditions for the growth of authoritarianism in the reign of Wilhelm II and, later, Nazi Germany. The tradition it maintained was not that of Liberalism, but that of the philosopher **Hegel**, who glorified the Prussian state as the ultimate human development. For **Wilhelmine** and Nazi writers, this tended to increase Bismarck's status as hero: for them, he saw through the 'weakness' of Liberalism. However, for the historians who deplored the militarism that developed after Bismarck's fall, and who were horrified at Nazism, the opposite was true. However much Bismarck's skill might be admired, the end results – and what subsequently happened – made him an **antihero**. Golo Mann, a German historian who had suffered under the Nazis, wrote furiously about the state that Bismarck had created in his book *The History of Germany since 1789* (1968):

'Like a speck of grease in a plate of soup, the pompous Imperial regime floated on the stream of prosperity created by others.'

This represented a view that saw the Empire as something unwholesome, false and alien, which sucked the wealth out of the German people – not something that was natural and beneficial to the people.

How realistic is the idea that Bismarck set Germany on a 'special way' to destruction?

A school of thought emerged in the 1960s and 1970s, particularly among German historians associated with the University of Bielefeld, in Germany. It was led by Hans-Ulrich Wehler in his book *The German Empire* (1975), which saw Germany pursuing what was called, in German, a *Sonderweg*. This means 'special way'. In essence the argument is that there was huge economic growth in Germany after about 1850, but that this, ultimately, did not lead to the middle-class, liberal state it should have. Rather, it set Germany on a unique path to a self-destructive, illiberal future.

The extended version is that, after 1850, railways and heavy industry ensured Prussian economic domination and contributed to her military victories. Unification in 1871 in turn stimulated more growth. Heavy industry and urban growth characterised German development after 1871. However, political development lagged behind. The assumption often made that industrial development would increase the power of the middle classes and lead to liberalism proved wrong. Instead, a feeble parliament never gained power appropriate to its wealth and economic importance. A militaristic, aristocratic and reactionary state remained.

In terms of technical knowledge, science and industry, Germany steamed ahead. In material matters it progressed: its welfare state was more advanced than that of any other country; its cultural achievements, particularly musical, were enormous. But its contempt for freedom, integrity, and the views and rights of others increased, and it remained stunted, rooted in the past. The argument concludes that these tendencies caused fatal tensions within the state, a major war in 1914, the failure of democracy after 1918, the rise of Nazism, and division during the Cold War. *Sonderweg* historians today claim that those same tendencies are still making problems for Germany in the twenty-first century.

Did Bismarck really make Nazism inevitable?

Not surprisingly, there have been challenges to this interpretation by historians like Thomas Nipperdey in *German History 1866 to 1918* (1990). Its principal critic has been Lothar Gall, a German historian who has introduced the concept that Bismarck was a 'white revolutionary' (see **Landmark Study**, p. 36). Gall tries to analyse Bismarck not in a Nazi context, but in an earlier context. He stresses the elements of compromise in Bismarck's approach to parliament. He also stresses Bismarck's shift from uncompromising opponent of Liberalism to statesman who, whatever his personal feelings, recognised the significance of many Liberal ideas and of compromise. The result was a revolution in German life that contained many progressive elements. It was by no means inevitable that Bismarckian Germany should develop into a Nazi tyranny.

Lothar Gall, *Bismarck, The White Revolutionary* (Allen and Unwin, 1986)

Post-war historians tended to see Bismarck as fundamentally illiberal and pick up on the hostile views of liberal opponents. The Prussianisation of Germany, the restricted role of the Reichstag, the labelling of opponents as 'enemies of the Reich', and the manipulation of foreign policy to domestic ends had built up a picture of a precursor to Hitler. Adapted by the Bielefeld school with their view of Bismarckian Germany being a 'special way', this seemed to take Bismarck out of his nineteenth-century context and examine him through the lens of twentieth-century experience. Gall picked up the paradox of a reactionary personality nevertheless creating a new Germany. The title of his book plays with these concepts: Wilhelm I once described Bismarck as a 'red reactionary' – he was prepared to use bloodshed ('red') to stop change and progress ('reactionary'). Yet Gall identifies him as a 'white revolutionary'. White is traditionally the colour of those opposed to revolutionary change, and the political opposite of red. By linking 'white' to 'revolutionary', Gall indicates that, despite his conservative views, Bismarck did bring about significant political, economic and social change. His image of Bismarck as a 'sorcerer's apprentice', unwittingly unleashing forces that proved beyond his control, is very powerful. It is a valuable concept that can be applied to many aspects of his policy after 1871 without underplaying his considerable domestic achievements.

How did Bismarck change from 'red reactionary' to founder of the 1867 constitution?

The Indemnity Bill of 1866

By 1847, Bismarck's reputation as a man of iron will had been enhanced by his refusal to budge over his defence of army reform. He seemed to be completely undermining the constitution. Yet he did not launch a coup; neither did he reject the whole idea of a parliament. Moreover, at the moment of his greatest triumph in 1866 – Prussia's victory over Austria – he went out of his way to build bridges with his previous enemies by introducing an Indemnity Bill. This gave legality to the taxes he had collected without parliamentary consent.

Bismarck and the winds of change

Was this Bill a cynical ploy aimed at getting his previous enemies to support him, or was Bismarck moving with the times? Like it or not, the forces of nationalism and Liberalism were here to stay. Even the heir to the throne (the future Frederick III) was sympathetic to them. Education and economic development had meant that the Germany of 1848 was very different from the Germany of 1866. So was Bismarck. Since 1848 he had seen more of the world, read more, considered more, met a wider range of people. Would some development not be expected? Indeed, he made clear his changed position in a paper on the question of unifying the German peoples, intended for the King in 1861. He wrote that there should be 'national representation of the German people at the centre of the Bund'. The Zollverein should also have a new parliament

Against this more progressive attitude must be set the tactless handling of parliament, petty persecutions and censorship, and his famous desire to punish the city council of Frankfurt for hosting a liberal national assembly against his wishes in 1865. However, the fact remains that many former Liberal opponents (though by no means all) did swing to support him in 1866.

Criticisms of the 1867 and 1871 constitutions – were they a 'fig leaf for absolutism'?

Indictment: a criticism, negative judgement, or accusation.

Historian Geoffrey Barraclough summed up the **indictment** of the constitutional arrangements of 1867 and 1871 in his work *Factors in German History* (1946). His case was that federal rights were illusions – they existed only on paper. Prussia could always veto constitutional changes because of the huge number of Prussian deputies in the Reichstag. The Chancellor was not obliged to consult anyone except the King of Prussia, who was also Emperor. The Reichstag was elected by universal male suffrage, but had no power of voting or refusing to vote taxes – the central government revenue was provided by permanent fixed duties or contributions from individual states. The Reichstag had no control over ministers. They were responsible only to the Emperor-King. According to Barraclough, the system was 'a veiled form of **monarchical absolutism** vested in the King of Prussia'. The conjuring trick that Bismarck had performed was to divorce Nationalism from

Monarchical absolutism: the belief that all power should be in the hands of the king or queen.

Bismarck with a group of deputies in the Reichstag that he created, 1871.

Liberalism, and in the process Liberal development was blocked. For Barraclough, this was what set Germany on course for a greater type of legal tyranny – that of the Nazis.

Factors in favour of the constitutions

There are, however, objections to this argument. The rules of the Constitutions are there for all to see, but it is their interpretation that can be open to discussion. A big factor to take into account is the constitutional background and experience of the other German states. The political systems and constitutions of these states had been developing independently, in some cases, since 1815. They were not necessarily subsumed into the Prussian system, and there is a case for seeing the North German Confederation as a highly successful compromise. The Reichstags of the Confederation and the Empire were able to pass a whole series of unifying measures. There was a national currency, a unified postal system, standard weights and measures, a liberal national industrial code, elimination of the last vestiges of internal customs barriers. These measures supported the development of modern business. There was specialist legislation that legalised bills of exchange, freeing large businesses and banks from the control of the state. Lothar Gall has called these processes 'an expression of a highly realistic understanding of the ways things were going economically, socially and politically', and views parliament as working – not being merely a sham. To see the Reichstag, elected by the people, as achieving nothing but frustrated criticisms is, perhaps, not entirely justified.

What was Prussia's role in federal Germany?

On the other hand, it cannot be argued that Prussia was an equal partner: with two-thirds of German territory under its control it could hardly be that. Seventeen out of 43 seats on the federal council created in 1867 were taken by Prussia. This was enough to stop any state gaining the necessary two-thirds majority to change the constitution. Prussia controlled the foreign policy and defence of the Confederation, and later the Empire. In the light of Prussia's victories, this was inevitable. However, federal laws (as opposed to constitutional change) needed only a simple majority in the federal council and could not be vetoed by Prussia. Legal jurisdiction, and matters of religion and education, were left to the states. When Bavaria joined the Reich it negotiated maintaining an independent army (except in war) and diplomatic representation abroad. Bismarck also allowed the Bundesrat to be responsible for declaring war.

The freedom of the states in the North German Confederation

A vital point that is not always grasped by students or discussed in textbooks is that the political life of Germany was not all focused on the federal parliament. Comparing the German system with the English model is not always helpful. The American federal system provides a fairer comparison. There were many internal matters left to the states in both systems. Eric Dorn Brose in *German History 1789–1867* (1997) has said of Germany that, 'The historical force of **particularism** was far too important to allow Prussia a dominant position in the new federal structure'. David Blackbourn's *Germany 1780–1918: The Long Nineteenth Century* (1997) compares certain aspects of 'liberal' Britain and its empire unfavourably with those of the new Germany. However, against the universal suffrage and the need for all federal legislation to be approved by parliament were other factors: the lack of financial leverage through reliance on indirect taxes and the lack of control over the defence budget, which was voted only every seven years; and the domination of the national government by Prussia.

Particularism: belief that local/regional rights should be maintained against central government.

Much depended on how the system might develop. Here again there is disagreement. Did Bismarck envisage development? Perhaps he dreaded it or was indifferent to it, but the answer must be 'yes', given the fact that the heir to the throne, Frederick III, was a Liberal sympathiser. No one could have foreseen in 1871 that Frederick's reign would be so short when it finally came in 1888, or that his son, Wilhelm II, would pursue much less liberal policies.

How liberal were Bismarck's religious and social policies?

The National Liberals seemed to tie themselves to Bismarck and are often accused of selling their liberal beliefs for national expansion. The somewhat grovelling tone of National Liberals' praise for Bismarck reads uneasily. Yet the trade was not entirely one way. The new Germany did incorporate Liberal views, particularly in terms of economic development, and there is at least a case for seeing political development as also having Liberal elements. What is confusing in a twenty-first-century context is this Liberalism pursuing somewhat illiberal policies in some matters.

The Centre Party and religious division

The episode of the Kulturkampf seems perhaps the most bizarre development of the new Germany. The process of unification had given Prussia more Catholic subjects and added Catholics to the Reich as a whole. This had created problems because religious intolerance had increased: Papal hostility to nationalism and liberalism was strongly expressed and was resented by Protestant opinion. Further, the Catholics in Germany had formed a political party to defend their rights. This was the **Centre Party** – a popular special-interest party. In a way, this type of party undermined Liberal notions of parliamentary government, as it was not interested in Germany as a whole, but only in the rights of one group – Catholics. It was also associated with **localism**, particularly in Hanover, where anti-Prussian feeling found an outlet. The Centre party leader **Ludwig Windthorst** grieved not only for Catholic rights in a largely Protestant state, but also for Hanover's former independence. The party was associated with an international body, the Roman Catholic Church, and with the illiberal views of the Pope, who had condemned notions of national unity, Liberalism and democracy as errors.

Centre Party: a German political party formed solely with the aim of defending the interests of German Catholics.

Localism: opposition to central/national government interference in local affairs.

Kulturkampf

The response of the Prussian state, and by extension the new Germany, was a campaign of anti-clericalism that was repressive and not liberal or in modern eyes ethical. Yet it seemed Liberal. The very word 'Kulturkampf' refers to a struggle between 'cultures', in the sense of world-outlooks or civilisations. If the modern world were to be free, scientific, rational, empowering the individual – and leading to material, artistic and spiritual progress – then it could not be held back by reactionary, unscientific, old-fashioned religious practices. Between 1871 and 1887 there was conflict between Bismarck and the Catholic Church. Bismarck disliked the influence of the decrees of the Vatican council on German Catholics as they seemed to interfere with the rights of German subjects, and he disliked the Centre Party. The Jesuits were expelled from the Reich and priests forbidden to refer to politics in their sermons. In Prussia Bismarck supported an anticlerical Minister of Culture, Adalbert Falk. The May Laws of 1873 established state control of education of the clergy, set up a Royal Tribunal for Ecclesiastical Affairs to undermine papal authority and allowed provincial governors to vet church appointments of parish priests. In 1874 the endowments of parish priests who protested could be

Ludwig Windthorst (1812–1891)
A Catholic lawyer from Hanover, Windthorst became a member of the Hanoverian Diet in 1848, speaking for Catholic interests. In 1851 he was appointed minister of justice. He resented the annexation of Hanover by Prussia in 1866, and from 1867 was a member of both the Reichstag and the Prussian Diet. He brought together deputies hostile to Bismarck, which led to the organisation of the Centre Party. Windthorst was its leader from 1874. He bitterly opposed the Kulturkampf and was an enemy of Bismarck.

confiscated and bishops who did not accept the laws could be imprisoned. Over a thousand Catholic parishes were left without priests, and 2412 clergy were arrested or imprisoned.

The philosophical aspects of the 'struggle' or the desire to placate Liberal parliamentary opinion probably did not concern Bismarck. He was more likely to be anxious about the implications of organised political Catholicism.

But, for whatever reasons, Liberal opinion and the Bismarck government joined in persecuting what Bismarck called **'enemies of the Empire'**. This was a somewhat ominous concept. Internal enemies would be fought – their ideas would not form part of an ongoing national debate, and differences would not be reconciled within a parliamentary structure.

'Enemies of the Empire' (*Reichsfeinde*): a special word used by Bismarck to attack his opponents – it made his critics appear to be attacking the whole German state and people.

The end of Kulturkampf

What is significant is that Bismarck did not persist in this Liberal illiberalism. The Centre Party was not crushed in the way that Hitler crushed opposition, and it became a part of the political system. As a civilised man of the nineteenth century, Bismarck could not persist with ever-more humiliating and somewhat ludicrous acts against priests and nuns. However, with the waning of the Kulturkampf, there was also the end of the alliance with the Liberals. Bismarck moved away from Liberal notions of free trade, towards a tariff that, in 1879, gave the Imperial government greater income, and therefore even greater independence from the Reichstag.

German socialism

Prussian traditions had more in common with German socialism than middle-class Liberalism: socialism believed in the role of the state, rejected **individualism** and was sceptical of parliament. The socialist philosopher Karl Marx was influenced greatly by the philosophy of Hegel, who held the Prussian state to be a sort of ideal. An interesting meeting took place between the socialist leader Ferdinand Lassalle and Bismarck in 1863. It was the universal suffrage that Bismarck introduced that made possible a much larger socialist party: the SPD – the Socialist Party of Germany, in 1875.

Individualism: the belief that the rights of the individual must be safeguarded and that individual enterprise was the key to economic growth and prosperity.

What was behind Bismarck's anti-socialist campaign?

The anti-socialist law of 1878 reflected Bismarck's fear of the socialists and an unfamiliar and threatening working class that had developed within the new Germany. The deputies were not to be

A *Punch* cartoon of 1878 commenting on Bismarck's anti-socialist law of the same year. It shows the Chancellor trying to suppress socialism, stuffing the 'socialist jack' back into its 'box'.

expelled from the Reichstag, but the Socialist Party constituency organisations were to be broken up, its press made illegal and socialist clubs and trade unions banned. The first time it was proposed by Bismarck, it was rejected by the Reichstag. Then an attempt was made on Wilhelm I's life by an ex-Socialist Party member that Bismarck eagerly seized upon. In June 1878 the Reichstag was dissolved and a hysterical anti-socialist campaign began. Bismarck seems to have relished putting the Liberals into the position of having to support more illiberal measures, but there was a certain logic. Class-based parties like the SPD did threaten the individual Liberal capitalism of the new Germany.

When Bismarck turned to more positive means of preventing working class hostility by passing social reforms, he was becoming more liberal, in a modern sense, but moving further away from the classic Liberal 'laissez-faire' position. These changes are of considerable significance and show that the new German state could be more flexible than its reputation as a precursor to tyranny suggests.

Social reforms

Bismarck was seen as 'killing Socialism by kindness' – cynically giving concessions to the workers purely for political motives.

Accident Insurance: an insurance scheme for working men to cover periods of unemployment due to accidents in the workplace.

However, he took up **Accident Insurance** with energy and even proposed nationalising the tobacco industry to pay for it. He passed the Health Insurance Act of 1883 based on 'best practice' of enlightened employers, enforcing health insurance on all low-paid salary and wage earners. The Accident Insurance Law followed in 1884. Contributions for health were divided between employer (33 per cent) and employee (66 per cent), but all contributions for the Accident Insurance came from employers. There was a considerable upsurge of interest in accident protection sponsored by the Imperial government insurance agency. In 1889 Bismarck wanted to go further in state financing of old age pensions than the Reichstag.

The historian Agnete von Specht, in her contribution to the Bismarck exhibition website of 1991 (www.dhm.de/ENGLISH/ausstellungen/bismarck) describes how Bismarck had depended on a civil servant, Lohmann, for the details of the measures, but that even he was critical on a fundamental level:

> 'Social discontent is not rooted in material grievances, but in working class demands for real equality before the law and a share in the achievements of modern culture.'

Bismarck focused on practicalities and had remarkably advanced views on the state's role in the welfare of the workers. Yet the moral and ethical arguments that formed the backbone of Liberalism – that in a modern state all classes need to feel a sense of equality and opportunity – probably eluded him.

The expulsion of the Poles

In a way, Bismarck's policy to the Polish subjects of the Empire reveals the extent of his liberalism. He wrote to his sister, 'Beat the Poles until they despair of living. If we want to survive we can do nothing but wipe them out'. He had two million Poles living in eastern Germany; their birth rate was rising faster than that of the German speakers. In February 1885, Bismarck ordered that Poles and Jews of Russian nationality be expelled from Prussia in a move that was, fundamentally, 'ethnic cleansing'.

Was Bismarck's Germany 'liberal'?

Most modern historians would agree with Edgar Feuchtwanger's description that the system established by Bismarck was 'semi-parliamentary' (*Bismarck*, 2002). Bismarck's political repression was obnoxious, but limited. The German state was not a dinosaur that did not move with the times, as both the growth of a federal system and the development of a modern social policy show. There was much that Bismarck did to modernise Germany that shows him to be far more than a blinkered Prussian Junker.

But, in the end, some crucial issues really must cast some doubt on whether Bismarck's Germany was really 'liberal': the huge growth in militarism and admiration for the policies of power and might; the disregard for the rights of the states annexed by Prussia in 1866; the resort to repression and to hysterical extra-parliamentary campaigns; and encouragement of rabid nationalism and even anti-Semitism when it suited.

Bismarck and Hitler?

Equally, though, the gap between the world of Bismarck and the world of Hitler is so huge – and contains a colossal world war of the type that Bismarck did everything to avoid – that comparisons between the Second and the Third Reichs must be handled with great care. Edward Crankshaw in his biography, *Bismarck* (1981), claimed that it was untrue to say that the Iron Chancellor was a forerunner of Hitler, or pursued policies which led inevitably to Hitler. Rather, he suggested the aspects of Germany that made it possible for Bismarck to rule for nearly thirty years were the same aspects that allowed Hitler to take and keep power sixty years later.

How Liberal was Bismarck's Germany?

1. Read the following extract and answer the question.

   'Unification has often been presented as a willing surrender by the Liberals. But that is one-sided and ignores those aspects of the process that Liberals could welcome. After all, anything that was disliked by Catholics and extreme conservatives was bound to have positive features in their ideas. Unification created a new constitution and a defined national state. The new Germany had much that was important for Liberals, the rule of law, freedom of movement, and a Liberal commercial code. They did not choose unity over freedom, but looked to extend freedom through unity.'

   (Adapted from David Blackbourn, *Germany 1780–1918: The Long Nineteenth Century*, Blackwell 2002.)

   'Bismarck destroyed German liberal hopes and paved the way for future dictatorship.' Using information from the passage above, and from the rest of this book, consider this view of Bismarck's domestic policy after 1871.

2. How far did Bismarck's domestic policy achieve its aims after 1871?

3

How successful was Bismarck's foreign policy after 1871?

Was he really Europe's 'master diplomat' before 1875?

How well did he deal with the crisis in the Balkans, 1875–8?

How effective were his policies after 1878?

Framework of events

1871	January German Empire proclaimed
	Treaty of Frankfurt: Alsace and Lorraine annexed by Germany; indemnity imposed on France by Germany.
1873	League of the Three Emperors (Dreikaiserbund) founded
	France pays off its indemnity to Germany
1875	'War scare' crisis with France
	Balkan revolt breaks out in Bosnia and Herzegovina
1876	Balkan crisis continues
1877	Russia declares war on Ottoman Empire
1878	Congress of Berlin
1879	Dual Alliance between Austria-Hungary and Germany
1881	Revival of Dreikaiserbund
1882	Italy joins Dual Alliance to form Triple Alliance
1884	Dreikaiserbund renewed
	German colonial expansion starts
1885	Crisis over Bulgaria
	Colonial expansion continues
1887	Reinsurance Treaty signed between Russia and Germany
1888	Mediterranean Agreements signed
1891	18 March Bismarck resigns as Chancellor
	Reinsurance Treaty not renewed
1894	Franco-Russian military alliance declared

Was Bismarck really Europe's 'master diplomat' before 1875?

Bismarck forged a network of alliances, intending to prevent conflicts. He was concerned to avoid any future war between Austria and Russia, and needed to keep France as isolated as possible. He became a supreme puppeteer, famously portrayed as such in a Punch cartoon of the 1800s (below). He favoured some controversial policies, such as the 'war scare' engineered against France in 1875, but the overall picture is one of a defence of peace. Henry Kissinger (US Secretary of State 1973–7) saw Bismarck as a **master diplomat**, and modern historians who are critical of his domestic policies – like Ernst Engleberg in *Bismarck* (1975) – nevertheless praise his diplomacy after 1871.

Master diplomat: someone so skilled in relations with other countries that he went beyond the normal statesman into a sort of diplomatic super star.

Essentially, Bismarck's diplomatic web of alliances had two main aims:

- to keep France isolated

- to keep Austria-Hungary and Russia from war by stressing their common interest with Germany in preventing revolution and change.

This cartoon, entitled 'The Three Emperors; or, The Ventriloquist of Varzin!', comments on Bismarck's control over the Emperors of Austria, Germany and Russia in the Dreikaiserbund (see p. 48). Varzin was Bismarck's Prussian estate.

Landmark Study The book that changed people's views

Imanuel Geiss, *German Foreign Policy 1871–1914* (Routledge, 1976)

After the praise for Bismarck as peacemaker, master diplomat and all-knowing moderate, the sourer judgements of this study are stimulating and invite a reconsideration of the policies. There has been a wide measure of agreement that Bismarck's successors berated Germany and undermined the wise and peaceful policies of Bismarck — based as they were on rational considerations of national interest rather than emotional concepts of national greatness. Even studies such as George F. Kennan's *The Decline of Bismarck's European Order* (1979), which have agreed that the Bismarckian system was trying to defend the undefendable, have given Bismarck more credit than Geiss. However, there is now a view that there was more continuity beween the pre-1890 situation and that which developed afterwards than has been previously thought. Moreover, there has been more focus on asking exactly what Bismarck was trying to defend. As with all important historical works, concepts are challenged and assumptions questioned.

As bad feeling grew between Russia and Austria-Hungary, so Bismarck had to resort to ever more complex diplomacy. He eventually allied with Austria-Hungary, but kept a separate agreement with Russia, whilst linking Britain to the alliances by supporting agreements to maintain the status quo in the Mediterranean, an area important to British trade and interests. The situation Bismarck left with his departure in 1891 was difficult to maintain and was not continued but, as Bruce Waller wrote (summarising the views of many other historians), 'the fault lay with the pygmies who succeeded him in high office' (*History Review No. 30*, March 1998). There is a view that, if only Bismarck's successors had kept his policies alive, Russia and France would not have allied, Britain would not have become an enemy of Germany, Austria would not have been encouraged to act rashly by invading Serbia, and the First World War might never have happened.

Not all historians share this favourable view of super-subtle manipulation. Paul Schröder in the *Short Oxford History of Europe* neatly summarises some of the critics' comments: 'It was a complicated, entangling and fragile system', which ended by 'no longer balancing existing antagonisms, but promoting antagonistic policies so as to balance them and keep Germany the arbiter'. The argument has been made – for example by critics like Imanuel Geiss in *German Foreign Policy 1871–1914* (1976; see **Landmark Study**, above) – that Bismarck's policies were just too complex and depended on Germany being in a position to settle crises. Such policies were not likely to be maintained on a long-term basis, and were dangerous and unsustainable by successors – whether 'pygmies' or merely responsible statesmen.

How did the new generation of Germans see Bismarck's policies?

Frederick (II) the Great (1712–1786)
'Old Fritz' was a homosexual militarist and one of the greatest generals of his age. He was King of Prussia from 1740 until his death. The brilliant manoeuvres of his troops relied on intense discipline. He succeeded in increasing Prussia's territory and sustaining wars against Austria and Russia in which Prussia was outnumbered. An 'enlightened despot' (tyrant), he introduced reforms in Prussia and became a hero to generations of nationalists.

Other problems were views that arose within Germany itself. These are analysed by Hans Kohn in *The Mind of Germany* (1960), and centre on many contemporary Germans seeing Germany as the first country of the world after 1871. Supposedly, the deeper insight and higher morality of the German mind gave it the right to more territory and influence. Without a dynamic policy of expansion that built on the Empire of 1871, there would be the appalling prospect the world dividing itself between the English-speaking nations and Russia. This set up a conflict between Bismarck and many in the younger generation. Bismarck was looking at the world through Prussian, not German eyes. His generation was conscious of the 1760s when **Frederick the Great** had faced a coalition of France, Austria and Russia that had all but overwhelmed him. But younger men and women were looking not at a time when Prussia had to be wary, forge alliances and use its resources with care. They were looking at the power of a new Germany with great factories, huge military forces tried and tested on the battlefield, with a belief in the greatness of its culture and its mental and moral outlook. Ironically, they were looking at these factors because of Bismarck's success; but increasingly his caution and pessimism were alien to their sense of mission and purpose. It was natural that they should see his policies as backwards-looking, and want to change them after his retirement.

The problem with France, and the Treaty of Frankfurt, 1871

Bismarck hoped to link Germany, Austria and Russia in a League of Three Emperors (Dreikaiserbund) in order to isolate France and prevent her allying with either power. The conservative image of the new Reich, it was hoped, would reassure the Tsar and the Austrian Emperor. They might be naturally hostile to a republic, whose interests could be seen as different to theirs. Britain seemed unlikely to join with France and would not oppose the League. The problem that Bismarck was trying to solve with this alliance was partly caused by his own policy. His policy in the Treaty of Frankfurt is often criticised. The French government that had emerged from the Franco-Prussian war, having overthrown Napoleon III in 1870, was a conservative one; its leaders had not been associated with Napoleon III's mistakes. Yet it was they who were punished by the Treaty, in which Germany had imposed a severe fine and annexed Alsace and Lorraine. These lands were not given the status of the other parts of the Reich, but remained a *Reichsland* – a virtual colony. This harshness only served to provoke dangerous nationalist movements within France. It ultimately prevented French statesmen having rational discussions with German leaders without incurring taunts of traitorous behaviour from their compatriots. It also led to the prolonged build-up of armaments and, eventually, in 1894, to the Franco-Russian alliance that Bismarck dreaded. Bismarck had tried hard to avoid this by stressing the shared interests of conservative empires like Germany and Russia to make a solid front against republican regimes.

The Dreikaiserbund, 1872

Bismarck was eager to protect Germany against any further French attack and negotiated this agreement between the three emperors of Austria-Hungary (Franz Josef), Germany (Wilhelm I) and Russia (Alexander II) in 1872. Despite the prevalent interpretation that Bismarck founded the League purely to isolate France, some historians – like William Langer in his influential *European Alliances and Alignments* (1931) – have argued that this attempt to secure monarchical solidarity was a rational defensive strategy to protect those monarchies against republican, nationalist and socialist uprisings. In this sense, it harked back to the volatile, revolutionary period before 1848. Yet this view ignores the fact that this type of protective stance was, in fact, out of date in the more conservative Europe of 1872. The possibility of conflict in Eastern Europe and the Balkans was growing. The foundation of the Dual Monarchy drew Austria's attention eastwards. Russia showed growing interest in Pan Slav nationalism and had rejected restrictions on her navy operating in the Black Sea.

Again, Bismarck was trying to solve problems that he had helped to create. The new Germany was an influential power. Russia would now look for its support in any quarrels with Austria-Hungary because Russia had not intervened when Bismarck was making the new German Empire. Austria would look for German support as a fellow German-speaking power. If either power was disappointed, there was the danger that it might ally with France. Bismarck relied on common political ideas between the three emperors – the trick that had worked earlier that century to keep nationalism down. However, this policy enjoyed only limited success: the Dreikaiserbund was renewed in 1874, but then lapsed until 1881. It was renewed again in 1884, but by the end of the 1880s it had become a dead letter. It did little to stop hostility between Austria and Russia over the Balkans. Whether the Dreikaiserbund was realistic or merely nostalgic is a matter for debate.

The 'war scare', 1875

By 1873 France had paid off the indemnity imposed by Germany, and seemed to be recovering. Yet, in March 1875, Bismarck stopped the export of German horses to France, and in April he started a press campaign in Germany that involved an article entitled 'Is War in Sight?'. This looked like typical Bismarckian brinkmanship. That he provoked a problem with a view to seeing what advantage might result may shed light on his methods and personality. A. J. P. Taylor (*The Struggle for Mastery in Europe*, 1954) linked it to a desire to draw attention away from domestic problems and the failures of the Kulturkampf in Germany. But this 'war scare' yielded only criticism both at home and abroad. Both Britain and Russia expressed alarm at this new German hostility to France. Edgar Feuchtwanger (*Bismarck*, 2002) offers the defence that the crisis allowed Bismarck to see where he stood in Europe. However, it was clear that France had gained the most: she had paid her fine, built up her army, and now gained European sympathy from what seemed like bullying. Bismarck had to back down and claim that there was no crisis. What was clear now was that the provocative methods employed in the 1860s in order to test reactions and gain advantage would not continue to work. Bismarck was forced to consider whether firm alliance in Europe was necessary, and the incident may have been a stepping-stone towards the alliance with Austria-Hungary in 1879.

How well did Bismarck deal with the crisis in the Balkans, 1875–8?

Bismarck was fairly sure of what he hoped for as a result of the Balkans crisis (see opposite). He wrote to his son in 1877, saying that Russia would need Germany as an ally. Antagonism over the Balkans would prevent Russia and Austria getting together for an 'anti-German conspiracy'. Above all, if attention shifted to Eastern Europe, it would be to Germany's advantage because its possession of Central Europe would not be challenged. This detached view was possible because there were no direct German interests involved.

The Balkans and the Eastern Question

In 1875 a revolt broke out in the Balkans (see map, p. 52). Bosnia and Herzegovina rebelled against their ruler, the Ottoman (Turkish) Empire. The revolt aroused the interest of Europe and began an episode that became known as the 'Eastern Question'. Austria-Hungary wanted to take Bosnia and Herzegovina for itself to stop Russian expansion into the Balkans. Britain wanted to stop any Russian expansion into the Mediterranean that might threaten its interests in the Suez Canal and the route to its prize colony, India. France wanted to use the crisis to re-establish itself as a great power by taking part in decisions with other powers.

Yet these powers failed to negotiate a peace between Turkey and the rebels, and the revolt spread to Bulgaria, with independent states Serbia and Montenegro joining in against Turkey. This extended revolt was suppressed by Turkish troops, and there were reports of considerable atrocity and deaths. This is what was referred to in England as 'The Bulgarian Horrors'. Feelings in Russia, where there was a desire to protect Christian Slavs, ran high.

At first, it seemed that Austria and Russia would maintain the friendly spirit of the Dreikaiserbund and stay out, but pressure was too strong, and by November 1876 Tsar Alexander II of Russia was speaking of Russia's mission to intervene. Russia got approval from the other powers for a reform programme giving self-government to Bulgaria, and in 1877 went to war against the Turks to enforce it. Russia was expected to sweep through Turkish territories and take Constantinople. However, its forces were held up by the Turks at the fortress of Plevna, saving the Ottoman Empire and preventing a general European war. Russia and Turkey agreed to peace and, at the Treaty of San Stefano in March 1878, created a new state of Bulgaria. This went beyond Russia's 1877 proposal, and it seemed that Russia had created a **client state** in the Balkans that would allow her to dominate the whole area.

Britain took the lead in opposing this and, by military threats, got a secret agreement to divide Bulgaria, keeping part as a Turkish province. These proposals formed the basis of a treaty signed at the international Congress of Berlin, hosted by Bismarck in July 1878. Bulgaria was divided into three: a new state of Bulgaria; a semi-autonomous Turkish province, Eastern Rumelia; and Macedonia, which remained firmly under Turkish rule. Britain gained Cyprus. Russia gained the province of Southern Bessarabia and the Ottoman port of Batum. Austria occupied Bosnia and Herzegovina. Germany gained nothing but the prestige of hosting the conference as an 'honest broker'.

Client state: a state that is nominally self-governing, but in practice dominated by a more powerful country.

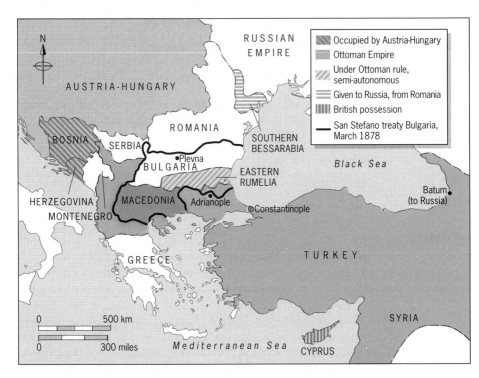

The Balkans after the Congress of Berlin, July 1878.

Could Bismarck and Germany really be detached from the Balkans crisis?

Yet there was some self-deception in the analysis that no direct German interests would be involved. Essentially it saw the possibility of Bismarck standing aside – the 'honest broker' – without this having serious consequences for Germany. Indeed, Bismarck's banker, Bleichröder, sourly pointed out that in the world of business 'there is no honest broker' – there is always a price to be paid for any transaction, and no broker is ever strictly impartial. In this case, Bismarck could not afford to be strictly 'honest'. This would mean paying his debts to Russia, who had stood back and allowed Prussia to emerge as a strong power. Now it was Russia's turn: she needed Bismarck's support in the Balkans. But he would not give it. No German statesman could have allowed Russian power to grow there. It would have been impossible to abandon Austria and to allow a large pro-Russian Bulgaria to dominate the Balkans. Such a policy would have brought the hostility of Austria and Britain. In the background was France eager for allies and ready to support a revived Crimean War alliance of Austria, France, Turkey and Britain against Russia. Also, the Russian threat to Austria was really a threat to Germany as well.

However, to oppose Russia completely would have been to undermine the Dreikaiserbund policy of 1872–5, which wanted Austria and Russia kept together to avoid either joining France. And France would be only too willing to join a disgruntled Russia after the 'war scare' of 1875. What Bismarck apparently saw as a situation ripe with all sorts of possibilities was in fact a potential nightmare. The old Prussia might well have stayed out of the situation, but Imperial Germany as a Great Power had to be a major influence in the international crisis.

Did the Congress of Berlin bring Bismarck what he wanted?

So, on the surface, Bismarck played his diplomatic part on the world stage with great effectiveness. Much of the work was done prior to the Congress of Berlin, so that the whole event could be a glittering occasion worthy of Berlin's new image. Bismarck's charm was put to work on the ministers and dignitaries, whom Germany's new rail network brought to the capital. This was to be a new type of diplomacy, characterised by less formality than past conferences. Huge meals and a hearty, down-to-earth German manner won over some, if not all of the delegates. The British leader Disraeli was more charmed than the French and Russian representatives. Utterly indifferent to the feelings of the Bulgarians, the people of Cyprus, or the national feeling in the Balkans, Bismarck was concerned only with trying to restore and maintain as much of the status quo as possible. However, in reality this was not possible. Russia had been alienated by Germany's failure to support her. No permanent Balkan settlement emerged. By 1879 Bismarck had moved to a new policy that was to change the fate of Europe: he had decided on an alliance with Austria-Hungary.

How effective were Bismarck's policies after 1878?

What was the Dual Alliance?

The Dual Alliance between Germany and Austria-Hungary (1879) became the start of a series of entangling alliances and pacts that was one of the major causes of the First World War. The pact, which was partly secret at Austria-Hungary's wish, named Russia as a potential enemy. If either power were to be attacked by Russia, the other was committed to war. If they were attacked by any other power, the only commitment was benevolent neutrality. This meant, for instance, that if France attacked Germany, all Austria-Hungary need do was be sympathetic to Germany; it need not fight. Because the terms of the pact were not made public, suspicion in Russia and France was inevitably aroused.

What was behind it, and what did it mean?

At the time, the danger of a revival of the Crimean War alliance of Austria, France and Britain seemed real. Perhaps an alliance with Austria-Hungary could be turned to force Austria-Hungary into better relations with Russia, thus stopping both countries allying with France. Also, alliance with Austria would bring closer relations with Britain and, since most Austrians were Catholic, help Bismarck improve relations with his Catholic subjects and put an end to the Kulturkampf.

Bismarck claimed an alliance would have other advantageous effects, too. He told Wilhelm I that it would be protection from Russia and would repair the damage done to Germanic unity by the war of 1866. He told Britain that the alliance would halt Russia's expansionism, and told Russia that it would weaken Austrian links with Britain. Bismarck appeared to be highly persuasive, totally in control and aware of every possible eventuality. However, less favourable interpretations of his foreign policy condemn him for the alliance. Imanuel Geiss's *German Foreign Policy 1871–1914* (1976) argued that Bismarck was committing Germany to an unrealistic policy of supporting an outdated Austro-Hungarian Empire, losing freedom of diplomatic manoeuvre and gaining little in return. Additionally, in retrospect, it seemed only a matter of time before Russia joined France and created the **encirclement** that Germany had always dreaded. From a position of being able to maintain independence in Balkan affairs, it now seemed that Germany would be sucked into minor quarrels through her allegiance with Austria-Hungary.

Encirclement: the fear that Germany would be surrounded by enemies and have to fight a war on two fronts.

Why did relations between Russia and Germany worsen after 1878?

Following the Congress of Berlin, Bismarck was aware that a resentful Russia was increasingly discontent with Germany. She began negotiating with France; there were troop movements on the Russian/German border, in Poland; she was publicly hostile to a new German tariff of 1879 that hit her wheat exports. Russia also criticised the German decision not to hold a plebiscite in Schleswig (promised in 1864) to allow the largely Danish population to make a choice between Germany and Denmark. Alexander II sent an angry letter to Wilhelm I in August 1879 – a reminder that Russia still remembered the support given to Prussia in the 1860s, and that Bismarck had not repaid this over the Balkans in 1878. All this may have driven Bismarck onto what was a potentially dangerous course, and one that he did not seem to have foreseen before 1877. What followed can either be seen as more masterly manipulation or just increasingly hopeless efforts to patch up differences between his earlier partners in the Dreikaiserbund.

Why was the Dreikaiserbund renewed in 1881 and 1884 if Russia was the Dual Alliance's potential enemy?

The league between Germany, Austria-Hungary and Russia was renewed on 18 June 1881, despite declining relations. It was based on fears of change. Tsar Alexander II had been assassinated earlier in the year. Ludicrously, Bismarck portrayed Gladstone's new Liberal British government as dangerously radical, and there was talk of the need for monarchies to co-operate against wild revolution and socialism. The renewal is sometimes seen as a high point of Bismarck's diplomacy. Luigi Albertini wrote in *The Origins of the War of 1914* (1957) that this was part of Bismarck's overriding principle of defusing conflicts and maintaining peace. However, there was little likelihood of ending long-term clashes of interest between Russia and Austria, especially as the Austrians had the secret Dual Alliance pact of 1879 in their back pocket.

Italy joined the Dual Alliance in 1882, forming the Triple Alliance. This seems to support the view of Bismarck as conscientious peacemaker. In fact, he had encouraged French expansion into Tunisia. This upset Italy, who feared a French colony so near Sicily. For Italy, there was the prestige of being recognised as a power equal with the much more powerful Central European empires. For Austria, there was less danger of an attack by Italy. (Some Italian-speaking areas were still under Austrian control, and Italy wanted them back.) Thus, in the event of war with Russia, Austria could concentrate all her forces against her enemy without worrying about an attack from Italy. Italy was also an ally against France. Britain's interests were to support Austria against Russia, so it seemed that everything was tightly sewn up. In 1884 the Dreikaiserbund was renewed, which seemed to give additional reassurance.

Why did Bismarck change policy and adopt colonialism in 1884–5?

The problem in both domestic and foreign policy by the 1880s was that forces for change were becoming too strong to be resisted. Economic growth was transforming Germany and giving rise to new demands and a new nationalism, making old-fashioned, alliance-based diplomacy redundant. Though nationalists were pleased by a return to a sort of **'Grossdeutsch'** policy of alliance with Austria, they increasingly saw Germany restricted and hemmed in by British imperial power. They regarded Russian nationalism and ambition as a threat that needed to be met in the same way that the threat from France had been met in 1870. Now the nation called for expansion and a new destiny, but colonies and engagement with either British or Russian power were not on Bismarck's agenda.

'Grossdeutch': 'of Greater Germany'. (One that included Austria and southern, Catholic Germany.)

However, concessions had to be made, and in 1884 and 1885 there was a sudden spate of German colonial expansion. In March 1884 Bismarck backed a German colonialist in establishing interests in West Africa that later led to Germany administering the region. The German colonial empire became quite extensive. In Africa there was Togoland, the Cameroons, German East Africa (Tanzania) and German South West Africa (Namibia). In the Pacific, New Guinea was the largest possession among a number of islands.

There have been many other reasons mooted for Bismarck's change of heart: the need to gain popularity in Reichstag elections in the face of increasing support for the Socialist and Catholic parties (Hans-Ulrich Wehler, *Bismarck and Imperialism*, 1969); the desire to quarrel with Britain over colonies to undermine the pro-British liberalism of the Crown Prince Frederick (A. J. P. Taylor, *Bismarck, Man and Statesman*, 1958); and a desire to mark imperial Britain out as a common enemy of both Germany and France, thereby improving relations with France and decreasing the chance of war on two fronts (Werner Richter, *Bismarck*, 1962).

Why didn't colonisation continue?

Whatever the motive, historians agree on Bismarck's lack of sincerity in colonisation. His own words to the Prussian State Secretary in September 1884 were: 'The whole colonial business is a swindle'. Colonisation was not pursued much beyond 1885. The reasons for it became fewer: the French still wanted revenge, and the government that had discussed colonisation in such a friendly way with Bismarck fell in disgrace in 1885; in Britain, Gladstone fell from power, and Bismarck had no desire to provoke the new Conservative government. Germany was left with troublesome and not very valuable colonies, whose later maladministration brought her into disrepute. It also encouraged the view that Germany had the right to **'a place in the sun'**, which later caused conflict with Britain and was a contributory cause of the First World War. The few gains hardly satisfied contemporary aspirations and, like the 'war scare' of 1875, this episode is usually seen as one of the least successful of Bismarck's foreign policy.

'A place in the sun': famous phrase, associated with Wilhelm II's desire for colonies and world power status. It is usually seen as a contributory cause of the First World War because it led to naval expansion and Anglo-German rivalry.

Why was the Bulgarian Crisis of 1885 important?

By the mid 1880s the diplomatic system Bismarck had built was tottering. The Balkans lurched once more into crisis. In 1885 Bulgaria overthrew the divisions imposed in the treaty signed at the Congress of Berlin and took over Eastern Rumelia from Turkey. The ruler of Bulgaria, the German prince Alexander of Battenberg, ignored Bismarck's advice and approved the takeover. The Russians disapproved of Alexander because he was friendly with Britain. In 1886 Russia backed a coup that toppled him from the throne. There was now a danger that Russia would occupy Bulgaria, and Austria threatened armed intervention. Some wanted Germany to back Austria in a war against Russia. Bismarck stood against this, but the danger was clear – though the crisis was resolved, at any time in the future Austrian and Russian rivalry might provoke conflict.

Why did Bismarck sign the Reinsurance Treaty with Russia?

The danger of the 1879 alliance was apparent. Germany might be forced by circumstances to support Austria-Hungary in a conflict with Russia, opening the possibility of a war on two fronts if France took advantage. Bismarck now worked hard to avoid this war. He tried unsuccessfully to renew the Dreikaiserbund in 1887. Finally he was driven to a secret agreement with Russia, known as the Reinsurance Treaty. Both nations promised neutrality unless Russia invaded Austria or Germany invaded France. Germany promised support to Russia over Bulgaria. War was averted, and the treaty remained secret until 1896.

How effective was the Treaty in maintaining relations with Russia?

Critics within the German foreign office at the time saw the Treaty as unrealistic and over-complex, rather than a masterstroke. It had already been undermined in 1887 by the incident known as the *Lombardverbot*, which undermined financial dealings between German and Russian investors and businessmen. Increasingly, German generals, diplomats, businessmen and nationalists saw the future depending on firm alliance with Austria. Public opinion seemed to favour the Austrian link. In practical terms, if Russian ambitions in the Balkans threatened Austria, then it would be impossible, whatever complex arrangements had been made with Russia, for Germany to stand aside or return to being some sort of 'honest broker'.

Lombardverbot: when the German Imperial Bank refused to accept Russian stocks and shares as security for loans.

Bismarck's successors let the Reinsurance Treaty drop. They have been criticised as lacking the insight of the old Chancellor. However, there is a certain logic in their view. This has been stressed by George Kennan's *The Decline of Bismarck's European Order* (1979), which showed the increasing influence of Russian nationalism on Tsar Alexander III and his reluctance to continue the 1887 Reinsurance Treaty. By 1890, given the changes in the European situation, Bismarck's much-praised networks and alliances may have been unworkable.

Bismarck and the new Emperor

Since he had dreaded the accession of the liberal Frederick, the Crown Prince, Bismarck seemed to be lucky when the new Emperor died in 1888. However, his son Wilhelm II soon came into conflict with Bismarck, and the Iron Chancellor had little choice but to resign. Sometimes portrayed in terms of a dramatic confrontation between the wisdom and conservatism of age and the rash impetuousness of youth, this confrontation is often seen as unfavourable to the younger man.

What was Bismarck's legacy in foreign policy?

Interpretations favourable to Bismarck compare the actions of his successors unfavourably to his policies. The argument was established by early historians like Erich Brandenburg in *From Bismarck to the World War 1870–1914* (1927) that Bismarck's network of alliances were a brilliant means of keeping peace; that even his policy towards France became generous and conciliatory.

A famous *Punch* cartoon of 1890, entitled 'Dropping the Pilot'. Commenting on Bismarck's resignation, it shows Wilhelm II watching the Iron Chancellor leave the 'ship' of the German state, which he had guided for so long.

This was extended by subsequent admirers, such as William L. Langer in *European Alliances and Entanglements* (1931), and Luigi Albertini in *The Origins of the War of 1914* (1957). It became the normal view in famous school textbooks such as Denis Richards's *Modern Europe* (1938) that when Bismarck departed, moderation was abandoned: the Reinsurance Treaty was dropped; militarism was rampant; a fleet was started that provoked Britain; Germany became more politically repressive and linked more and more firmly with Austria; the desire for world power status and 'a place in the sun' led to ever more aggressive policies, which led to war and disaster.

This is to assume that Bismarck's policies were still successful by 1890 and not on the verge of collapse. The counter-argument is that events were outrunning Bismarck's ability to keep pace with them. In Imanuel Geiss's important *German Foreign Policy 1871–1914*, (1976), it is argued that Bismarck had sacrificed Germany's ability to pursue independent foreign policies for 'second-rate allies' – Austria and Italy. The alliance with Austria linked Germany to 'a political corpse'. The failure to establish first-rate allies like Britain or Russia was crucial. Even more sympathetic historians have agreed that during the 1880s, Bismarck was trying to defend a system that could not actually be defended indefinitely. George F. Kennan's important study *The Decline of Bismarck's European Order* (1979) agreed with the impossibility of trying to perpetually isolate France and support the multinational Austro-Hungarian state. The crucial feature for Kennan was the rise of Russian nationalism. It was Russian aggression and popular nationalism that undermined Bismarck's simple, logical and peaceful policy.

In a recent reappraisal, *Germany from Reich to Republic, 1871–1918* (2000), Matthew Seligman and Roderick McLean suggest that the major points of criticism of Bismarck's foreign policy after 1871 could be the decision to annex Alsace and Lorraine, which made a future friendship with France impossible, and also championing the survival of the Austro-Hungarian empire. Both these policies are linked with Bismarck's failure to engage fully with the forces of nationalism, whether it was Russian, French or German. They use the image of Bismarck as King Canute, trying in vain to stem a tide of national feeling. They agree, however, with A.J.P. Taylor's overall summary that Bismarck helped to give Europe peace for 40 years. To expect more may be unreasonable.

The irony was that Bismarck had relied heavily on manipulating public opinion and on the support of the Emperor in defending a Germany that rested on elite groups, the army, the wealthy middle classes and the aristocracy. Bismarck's foreign policy was out of step with these very groups. It is this, rather than the 'foolishness' of his successors, that may be considered the key to understanding the legacy of his foreign policy. It may also explain why the Reichstag that Bismarck himself had created greeted his resignation with icy silence.

Q How successful was Bismarck's foreign policy after 1871?

1. Read the following extract and answer the question.

   'Sceptical historians have described Bismarck's complex and contradictory alliance system as a conjuring trick. Bismarck had the simple and logical aims of both preventing an Austro-Russian war and discouraging either power from allying with France against Germany. However, as this involved an assumption of permanent French isolation and of close co-operation between Vienna, St. Petersburg and Berlin, it was unsustainable in the long run.'

   (Adapted from D. G. Williamson, *Bismarck and Germany 1862–1890*, Longman 1986.)

   'A policy that was based on reality and rightly aimed at peace.' Using information from this passage, and from the rest of the book, assess the view that Bismarck's foreign policy was highly successful in achieving his aims.

2. Explain why Bismarck opposed expansion in Europe, yet established an empire overseas.

Bismarck: an assessment

Was he the key to unification?

Bismarck the genius master-planner has been replaced in modern historiography by Bismarck the manipulator-of-circumstances. His true commitment to Unification has been the subject of debate. Economic development, military progress, and the particular diplomatic conditions of the 1860s may have given Bismarck advantages, but how he used them remains the key to understanding the emergence of a united Germany.

How Liberal was his Germany?

In unifying Germany, did the success of 'iron and blood' mean an unavoidable drift to authoritarianism? Did it lay the basis of Nazi Germany by undervaluing party politics and parliament? These may be distortions that examine Bismarck through the experience of Wilhelm II's and Hitler's Germany. There were Liberal elements in Bismarck's Reich and an expectation that these would develop.

How successful was his foreign policy after 1871?

Bismarck's mature and rational search for order and stability to protect the new Germany has often been compared favourably to the over-ambitious and dangerous policy of his successors. Yet Bismarck's policy arguably ceased to command support and meet changing circumstances before his fall. It has been seen as over-complex and unrealistic; like Bismarck himself it has been accused of inconsistency and cynicism.

Bismarck's legacy

The new Germany was of huge importance for the future. The emergence of a new state with powerful economic and military potential was to dominate European history. It could, in 1871, have been a force for progress and stability, or a cause of long-term instability and conflict. Again, Bismarck's cynicism was to have major consequences. German internal politics came to be dominated by parties representing religious, social or economic interests, and shifting coalitions, rather than by genuine political and constitutional growth. Material and scientific progress, and the unstoppable growth of militarism and nationalism, were the logical results of a country united by 'iron and blood'. In the end, it swamped the older and more traditional Germany that Bismarck loved and, ironically, destroyed.

Retreating to his estates with his dogs and peasants in 1890, Bismarck fretted in bitter resentment at the loss of a world dependent on personal power and influence to a new world of parliament, railways, industry and military power. It was the failure to reconcile these two worlds that was his legacy and, indeed, the subsequent tragedy of Germany.

Further reading

Texts specifically designed for students

Hargeaves, D. *Bismarck and German Unification: Documents and Debates* (Palgrave Macmillan, 1991)

Stiles, A. *The Unification of Germany 1815–90* (Edward Arnold, 1986)

Williamson, D.G. *Bismarck and Germany 1862–1890* (Longman Seminar, 1998)

Texts for more advanced study

Blackbourn, D. *Germany 1780–1918: The Long Nineteenth Century* (Blackwell, 2002) challenges critical views of Bismarck and liberalism.

Breuilly, J. *The Formation of the First German Nation-State 1800–1871* (Palgrave, 1996) looks at different interpretations of factors explaining unification.

Eyck, E. *Bismarck and the German Empire* (Norton, 1964) presents a hostile view that was influential in its day.

Feuchtwanger, E. *Bismarck* (Routlege, 2002) argues that Bismarck reacted to the circumstances of the time, rather than planning them, but takes a balanced view on his skills and creation of an illiberal Germany.

Gall, L. *Bismarck, The White Revolutionary* (Allen and Unwin, 1986) stands against the view that Bismarck was a forerunner of Nazi dictatorship.

Geiss, I. *German Foreign Policy 1871–1914* (Routlege, 1976) is unsympathetic to Bismarck's diplomatic methods.

McLean, R. and Seligman, M. *Germany from Reich to Republic 1871–1918* (Macmillan, 2000) summarises a wide range of the arguments.

Simon, W. M. *Germany in the Age of Bismarck* (Allen and Unwin, 1968) is a useful collection of documents, with a broad scope.

Taylor, A. J. P. *Bismarck: Man and Statesman* (Hamish Hamilton, 1958) is a groundbreaking study that challenges the previously accepted view that Bismarck had long-term plans for unification.

Index